CONTENTS

TO THE JEW FIRST:
THE FORMATION OF ONE NEW MAN

"God's ~~call of~~ purpose of mutual call &
" blessing "
PS. 130

MARTIN SHOUB

TO THE JEW FIRST: The Formation of One New Man

Copyright © 2017 by Martin Shoub

All rights reserved. No part of this book may be reproduced, distributed, or transmitted in any form or by any means, or stored in a database or retrieval system, without prior written permission from the author.

Unless otherwise noted, scripture quotations are from the ESV® Bible (The Holy Bible, English Standard Version®), copyright © 2001 by Crossway, a publishing ministry of Good News Publishers. Used by permission.
All rights reserved.
Scripture quotations marked (CEV) are from the Contemporary English Version Copyright © 1991, 1992, 1995 by American Bible Society. Used by Permission.
All rights reserved.
Scripture quotations marked NKV are taken from the New King James Version®. Copyright © 1982 by Thomas Nelson. Used by permission. All rights reserved.

Cover design by Elisha Isabelle Photography & Design
Cover photograph: "The binding of Isaac," Beit Alpha mosaic. Photography by Martin Shoub

ISBN: 978-154551169

Printed by CreateSpace, An Amazon.com Company

Dedicated to my loving wife Sue.

For her worth is far above rubies.
The heart of her husband safely trusts in her;
So he will have no lack of gain.
She does him good and not evil
All the days of her life.

FOREWARD

Marty Shoub is a mensch. It was my memorable opportunity to serve side by side with Marty in Israel at Tents of Mercy for eight years. There's no one I'd rather have represent our work in Israel on the world stage. I see him as a Messianic Jewish ambassador to the nations. He is also a treasured friend who has written a valuable book. Whether you are a newcomer to his subject or a seasoned teacher, you will find insight after insight of penetrating relevance, presented with real-time scholarship re: the Jewish-Gentile relationship in Messiah. The author's voice is personable, inviting us to hear the heart of God, to approach the Scriptures and history afresh, and to enjoy the exceptional fellowship our Lord. His inclusion of responses written by colleagues from the nations demonstrates gracious humility and the realization that our voices must rise together to proclaim our shared place in the olive tree of Romans 11.

My friend has tackled a subject that is too frequently misunderstood, yet is vital for the Body of Messiah to live out in a healthy way. We've not had this opportunity for at least 1800 years—to walk together as Jewish and Gentile disciples of Yeshua. Prior to 1967 this could not have happened, nor would a book like this have been written before that fateful year. In 1967 Jerusalem was restored as Israel's unified capital city, and Yeshua began capturing the hearts of Jewish hippies through the "Jesus movement." Since then there has been Jewish believers following Yeshua and continuing to live as Jews.

Throughout the history of the post-Jerusalem church, to believe in Jesus as Messiah, a Jew had to convert to

7

Christianity and disavow his/her Jewish identity. Now, indigenous congregations of Jewish believers in Yeshua exist throughout the world, including here in Israel. The native soil of the Gospel is again hosting a resurrected fig tree that has begun to blossom (Matthew 24:32-34). The Master gave this as a sign of his second coming.

Always many steps ahead of us all, the Lord has ever planned for the nations, no less than Israel, to participate in His Kingdom. Yet how this was to come about and what would be its implications for Israel—these are questions that have remained largely unanswered. Marty has tackled them and drawn clear understanding from the treasure chest of God's word; the depth of his teaching, yet the accessibility of his language makes this a valuable addition to the vital discussion of the relationship of Jesus' Jewish and non-Jewish disciples. As he states compellingly "In just the last 50 or so years the church of the circumcision has risen again from the ashes of history. Israel is back in the land promised to them by covenant and Messianic faith has been renewed in the land of Israel. Unlike previous generations, we are no longer hampered by circumstances. It is Messiah who creates One New Man but we are the generation that can avail ourselves of this opportunity."

My brother is calling for nothing less than a turning point in Church history. His message is that it is time for true Christians everywhere to welcome back their Jewish brothers and sisters, the original fathers and mothers of the entire worldwide movement for Jesus that began in Jerusalem. I am enthused to say AMEN!

As I escort you to begin reading, let me say that many books lack a "so what?" They end with no further action promised or proposed to the reader. "To the Jew First" supplies those steps of godly response for the reader whose heart is touched by the book's message. And it IS a book that calls for a response. How will you respond? I trust and pray that you will enter into the divinely authored process of restoring Yeshua's community to its fullness—Jew and Gentile, Israel and the nations. The King bids us prepare the way for His soon return. Let us seize the hour and boldly speak the truth in love.

Eitan Shishkoff
Tents of Mercy
Israel

PREFACE

The title of this book, "To the Jew First" may appear unsettling. To single out any group as somehow "first" and therefore special, grates against our assurance that no matter our background or status we are special too. From Sunday school on we are taught, "Jesus loves me, this I know" — the most basic truth of our relationship with God. The fact that Jesus loves me unconditionally as an individual removes any ethnic, racial, or economic privilege for any group of people.

And yet, in one of the most cherished and important books in the Bible, Paul begins his letter to the church in Rome by proclaiming the gospel is first to Jews and then to Gentiles (Romans 1:16). How are we to understand a priority distinction for Jews when Jesus himself told us he came to give his life because, "God so loved the world..."

Maybe, "First" is not about priority but chronology. That is, historically, first the gospel was for the Jews and over the course of time the gospel message shifted to the Gentiles. Unfortunately, this perspective is often lying underneath our understanding of God's plan of salvation. We might not have articulated it into a theological explanation but for many Christians, it colours our reading of the Bible as a story that begins with Israel's choosing and moves on to the plan of salvation for the nations of the world. There was a time when

11

almost all Christians believed this to be true. That is, the Church had replaced Israel as the object of God's love.

But, if we hold to the truth that God's love is for all, we still have a problem. How can God's love for the Jewish people ever pass on to someone else? Surely, the Gospel is still for Jews too. The promises in the Bible to the Jewish people are cast as emphatic declarations of eternal fidelity. As Isaiah explained, even a nursing mother, so naturally inclined to cherish and protect her child could perhaps, under the most distressing circumstances, forget the babe at her breast, but the God of Israel will never forget the descendants of Abraham, Isaac, and Jacob (Isa. 49:15).

This book assumes that replacement theology, the concept that the Church has replaced Israel as the people of God is not correct. There are many good books that refute replacement theology and I do not wish to rehash what others have so ably done. But because the belief that the Church has replaced Israel has been so entrenched in Christianity, even those Christians who reject this doctrine can still be subtly influenced by it. Because the vast preponderance of sermons, hymns, Bible studies and books written over the centuries have assumed the Church had replaced Israel, this doctrine has had a powerful influence on all believers — even on Messianic Jews (I speak from experience).

I hope this book will help us through the questions posed by this relationship between Jew and Gentiles. I have asked a number of my Gentile Christian friends and colleagues to comment on each chapter of this book. All these Gentile Christian contributors have been deeply touched by their own calling "to the Jew first". I want to thank all the contributors that added their thoughts and words to this book - especially my friend and ministry partner, Dean Bye.

Dean Bye is the director of Return Ministries, a Canadian, Christian Zionist organization that assists Jews returning to Israel, comforts new Israeli immigrants and challenges the Gentile church to embrace their call to participate in Israel's restoration. Dean and I often share a platform together as "One New Man". Many of the ideas I have communicated in this book I have learned from Dean. I wrote them down but Dean deserves credit for a good number of the ideas behind the words on these pages.

I am also indebted to Eitan Shishkoff. Eitan is the director of the Tents of Mercy network in Israel. He was my direct ministerial supervisor during my 8 year tenure with Tents of Mercy. Eitan's ideas are also reflected in my thinking. More then anyone, he first inspired me to consider the relationship between Jew and Gentile in the plans and purposes of God.

Throughout this book I have chosen to use the Hebrew name "Yeshua" rather than the English name "Jesus." My choice of using the name "Yeshua" over "Jesus" is in no way a slight or derogation against the more traditional English name for the Saviour. I choose to use His Hebrew name to emphasize His enduring connection to the Jewish people. Further, at times in the book, especially when I am making reference to the Hebrew name, YHVH - יהוה (translated in most English Bibles as "LORD"), I have used the common Jewish circumlocution "HaShem" (lit. "The Name"). As with the name Jesus, I do not have a theological problem with the term LORD, my choice of HaShem over LORD is for the same reason stated above.

13

I am a Messianic Jew. Like many of the first Jewish disciples I have been called to serve the Gentiles. All the other contributors are Gentiles who in some capacity have taken up their calling to serve the Jewish people. All of our spiritual journeys have led us to appreciate the beautiful symmetry and reciprocal blessings contained in God's plan for Jews and Gentiles. I could not have written this book by myself because the message of Jew and Gentile together in Messiah is best communicated by Jews and Gentiles together.

There are some things more appropriate for my friends to say as representatives of the Gentile church and other issues are best addressed by a Messianic Jew. Either way, we are affirming a love story conceived in the plan of God in ages past. Many Christians and Jews of all theological persuasions are recognizing that the enmity that has so marred relations between Christians and Jews is diametrically opposed to the heart of God.

Please join my friends and I as we explore what the Apostle Paul called a mystery – the redemptive plan in Jesus the Messiah for Jews and Christians to bless one another and thereby both receive a blessing.

INTRODUCTION

Marty's Story

A Jewish New Ager
from Montreal finds Messiah

I grew up in a traditional middle-class Jewish home in Montreal. My parent's generation was not especially devout or observant but Jewish identity was central to who we were. We were Jews and we stuck together. We were God's chosen people but that status meant little to me except as a barrier that separated us from those who were not the chosen ones. My family had cordial relationships with Gentiles but they were never part of our circle of friends, family and to some degree, even business associates. Jesus was the god of the Pope, the nuns I would see from time to time on city buses and the many grey stone churches dotted throughout Montreal. All I knew about him was that he was the source of untold troubles for our people down through the centuries. The sad looking man depicted on the crucifix statues in front of churches and cemeteries did not appeal to me. I had intuitively tapped into our people's long standing distrust and caution against Jesus, the Church and Christians. There is a well known saying among my people, "Stay away from *That Man*".

As a teenager I had a boundless curiosity to understand who I was and what life was about. I began to explore all sorts of alternate spiritual paths. I was open to everything and everyone -- everyone, except Yeshua. Despite my liberal outlook, the caution engrained in me through our people's collective distrust to "stay away from that man" was so deeply embedded I could not allow myself to seriously consider this man the Gentiles worshipped. Ironically, the more I sought for truth, the more I encountered the words of Yeshua, whether quoted out of context by an Indian guru or through the witness of well meaning Christians. The full story of how I came to faith in Yeshua as the Messiah is beyond the purview of this book. It is enough to recount that when I was nineteen years old I had a powerful encounter with the living God. I did not understand anything about Yeshua's sacrificial death on a cross, I had almost zero theological knowledge of the Christian faith, all I really knew was that I was wrong and God was right. The offer was simply, "Will you trust me with your life? Will you follow me?"

I said yes and my life changed in the most profound way. Truly, the best decision I ever made. As a Jew, two things changed for me. Looking back, one for the good and one that required correction. At once, I understood that the promises God made to Abraham were real, and I was part of an enduring legacy stretching back to Abraham, Isaac and Jacob. My Jewish back-story was not old fables but a reality that served to bless the whole world through Yeshua, the Messiah of Israel and saviour of the world. I also mistakenly, disassociated myself from that legacy. As I understood it, I was now a Christian. A Jewish Christian, yes, but that was no more significant than being an Italian Christian or a Chinese Christian or whatever ethnicity one might hale from. No more of this burden of being "The Chosen People". In Christ, all were one and ethnicity mattered not.

Of course, on one level this is absolutely true (See Gal. 3:28) but unfortunately, even as a Jew I accepted the narrative that the Church had replaced Israel as God's chosen. I was grateful for my background because it tied me to how my own people had been used by God in the past, but it no longer had significance for what God was doing in the present. None of the sincere Christians who first discipled me knew any better. As sincere as they were, they had no understanding for God's enduring faithfulness to Israel and how that faithfulness called me, a Jewish disciple of the Jewish Messiah to still live a Jewish life.[1]

My journey towards following Yeshua and living a Jewish life started over twenty years later. In 2000, I was receiving prayer from a pastor at our church's elders' retreat. As he finished praying for me, he looked at me and told me, "Don't be ashamed of your Jewish heritage." Truth be told, I was a bit put out. Who is he, a Gentile to tell me about my Jewish heritage? I am not ashamed (or so I had presumed). Still, his

---

[1] It was only many years later that I came to appreciate the words of Orthodox Jewish theologian, Michael Wyschogrod. He wrote that the "acid test" for whether Christians truly reject replacement theology is how they disciple Jewish Christians. If Christians believe that God's promises to Israel endure, then they will encourage Jews in the church to live a Jewish life. This view is ably supported by Messianic Jewish theologian, Mark S. Kinzer [Mark S.Kinzer, "Post Missionary Messianic Judaism" (Grand Rapids: Brazos, 2005) 181-212], and Christian theologian, R. Kendall Soulen [R. Kendall Soulen, The God of Israel and Christian Theology" (Minneapolis: Fortress, 1996) 1-21].

words remained with me and got me thinking. Was I ashamed? Did I really embrace my identity as a Jew? What did it mean for a Jew to follow the Jewish Messiah? I realized that I did not have the answers to these questions, and so began a quest to understand my calling as a Jewish believer in Yeshua.

I am still on this journey. The truth is, as we pursue the path to know Him, more and more, we come to know ourselves. I can tell you that just because I was born a Jew I did not possess any real advantage in understanding the scriptures free from the entanglements of replacement theology. Like everyone else, I "spiritualized" the Hebrew Scriptures so as to remove their significance and meaning as they related to the people who originally received them. I had to unlearn many assumptions based on the error of replacement theology too. I would never say I have arrived, but along the way I have re-discovered the scriptures as an incredible, marvellous and beautiful plan to see Jew and Gentile made one in Messiah.

Like any good relationship, blessings and responsibilities must flow both ways. A relationship where only one side gives and the other receives is either tragically co-dependent or sinisterly oppressive. Our Heavenly Father's plan brings mutual blessing, and mutual calling to both Jews and Gentiles, all to the praise of His glorious grace. Paul's gospel "To the Jew first..." is not a one sided relationship, but a beautiful love story that not only blesses both Jews and Gentiles but prepares the way for the return of Israel's king, the Saviour of the world.

Dean's Story

Saved to Make Israel Jealous

Dean Bye is my very good friend and ministry partner. We have given One New Man seminars together around the world. I have included Dean's biography as a separate chapter because it is so instructive as to how God calls believers on behalf of the Jewish people from among the Gentile Church.

Can the God of the universe speak to us through a license plate? The Scriptures record Him speaking through angels, the heavens, and a burning bush - even a donkey. I'm convinced if God finds a listener, He'll choose many ways to get his or her attention. One of the most significant, life-changing revelations I ever received began with a license plate fasted to the back of a car passing me on the highway at 120 kph.

But let me digress for a moment. It was 1991; my wife Patty and I were on the road, heading to Edmonton. The musical interlude on my car radio announced it was time for the six o'clock world news. The radio gave an update on the rapid decline and dissolution of the USSR. The Soviet empire was fragmenting into pieces at shocking speed. The news bulletin reported that now Estonia had followed Lithuania in breaking away from the once mighty super power. Every week around 1,500 Soviet Jews were leaving the former Russian republics. Many had hoped to begin a new life in Israel, free of communism, free to take hold of their birth-right, be Jewish in a Jewish state.

I began to ask myself who could have foreseen or predicted these times when the Jews in the nations would return home to Israel, and of all places, from behind the Iron Curtain of communist Russia? It had to be God. He appeared to be shaping world events in order to fulfill the prophetic Scriptures, and what's more, this was all taking place in my lifetime!

> *"Therefore, behold, the days are coming," declares the LORD, "when it shall no longer be said, 'As the LORD lives who brought up the people of Israel out of the land of Egypt,' but 'As the LORD lives who brought up the people of Israel out of the north country and out of all the countries where he had driven them.' For I will bring them back to their own land that I gave to their fathers."* (Jer. 16:14-15)

Due north of Jerusalem is Moscow. A great exodus of Jews 'from the north country' was happening for the entire world to see. The news agencies dutifully reported on these events but they were not equipped to relate these momentous changes to the prophetic fulfillment of the word of God. Pondering these thoughts, I wondered if God had something for me to do. Then it happened. A car sped past me on the highway and the license plate caught my attention: **ROM 1111.** I immediately thought of the scripture, Romans 11:11. The chatter on the radio began to fade as my attention was diverted. Within seconds my Bible laid open across the steering wheel as my curiosity compelled me to know what that Scripture said (Please remember this was 1991, I no longer drive and read the Bible at the same time). I sensed that God was about to speak to me about new direction and purpose for my life. Glancing at the page I read the following words:

"So I ask, did they stumble in order that they might fall? By no means! Rather through their trespass salvation has come to the Gentiles, so as to make Israel jealous."
(Rom. 11:11)

I was flabbergasted, "God, what do you mean 'I'm saved to make Israel jealous?'" Who had ever heard of such a thing, that I, a Gentile, owed my salvation to the Jews, that I am obligated to make them jealous? Was there any other Scripture that gives such a clear word about the purpose and destiny of why Gentiles have been saved?

Arriving home I asked Patty what she thought about how the Gentiles were to make jealous. My dear Patricia appeared to ignore my question, preoccupying herself with getting dinner completed and the children ready for the babysitter so we could leave for our Bible study. Perhaps she was also dealing with thoughts about her husband, whom she was faithfully committed to for better or worse, now claiming that God put a message on a license plate for us today. She may have been wondering if God enlisted angels to drive cars on highways with license plate messages. Little did we know then that this very message would be the motivating factor for our family for all the years to come.

21

After we arrived at Bible study I read out Romans 11:11 to the group. I followed up the scripture verse with this question: "If we are saved to make Jewish people jealous, how do we get on with God's plan? Then I added, "Is it not a sin to make someone jealous?"

Those questions led into an evening of discussion that stirred in us a responsibility to help the Soviet Jews making Aliyah to Israel. We wondered how long before the Jewish people of North America would glorify God's name by returning to their ancient homeland. At the end of the evening, the pastor leading the study suggested we all go to a conference the following week. The conference was entitled, "The Glory of Israel and the Church." What were the chances?

The conference turned out to be life changing for us as we learned many things about what God was doing with Israel and the Jewish people today. Israel had only become a nation in 1948. A land forsaken and desolate was now blooming like a rose, just like the prophets foretold. And now, even secular news outlets were reporting on this exodus coming out of Russia. Jews were leaving the former Soviet Union in great numbers as a direct fulfillment of many words the prophets had spoken.

We also learned that Christians were mobilizing to do their part, as was also prophesied. We realized that just by yielding to God's plans for Israel and the Jewish people, we could participate in making Israel jealous. Those attending the conference were given opportunity to bless, comfort, and help the Jewish people home to Israel with their finances. We were blessed to participate in this tremendous opportunity to fulfill the word of God and begin to make Israel jealous through righteous actions.

As long as I can remember, Jewish people had been in my life. They were my doctors; my dentist; my father's boss; one of my first jobs was selling ice cream as a teenager for a Jewish businessman. After college, I began a business that served many Jewish clients. For over 30 years of my life I never knew that God had a plan built right into my life, written and inscribed in Scripture. He wanted me to serve His precious Jewish people – not to grow my own business but to serve His Kingdom purpose. I had been ignorant of the role His people Israel were to play regarding the redemption of all mankind.

I was unaware of God's plan for Gentiles like me to serve them. It was time to step into my calling. It was time to agree to God's purpose in my life and begin to participate in provoking the Jews to jealousy, a jealousy for those things God is jealous for. I was receiving God's spirit of jealousy or zeal to do so. It was His zeal that was burning inside of me.

Romans 11:11 was a message from the Lord at a time when I needed to choose His purpose over my own. This one remarkable verse taught me why God had saved me. It also gave me, a Gentile believer in Jesus Christ, a distinct purpose for my life. As a Gentile, I have been saved to make Israel jealous! I can testify that almost 20 years later, this purpose has brought greater fullness in my life, my family and my extended family in the Lord. His great plan has always been that His chosen people, the Jews, would be made jealous by a people (the Gentiles) who were originally not His people, but now are His people (Deut. 32:21).

These Gentiles from the nations would do works of righteousness that would reveal that they were in fact worshippers of the one true God of Israel. This would provoke the Jewish people to return to their God, His Kingdom and His righteousness. It is not just the Jewish people that are chosen, I too have a high calling and have been chosen to be part of His plan that is all about exalting His great name through His people made jealous. The final outcome of this incredible plan is none other than world redemption!

CHAPTER 1

Paul's Revelation of the Gospel

In John's farewell discourse Yeshua promises his disciples that after his ascension the Holy Spirit would reveal further truth that they were not yet ready to receive:

> "I still have many things to say to you, but you cannot bear them now. When the Spirit of truth comes, he will guide you into all the truth, for he will not speak on his own authority, but whatever he hears he will speak, and he will declare to you the things that are to come." (John 16:12–13)

Yeshua had also stated "the first shall be last and last shall be first." In keeping with this promise there is some irony that the chief recipient of those truths the disciples could not bear was Shaul of Tarsus (a.k.a. the Apostle Paul) – a Pharisee of Pharisees, a disciple of the eminent rabbi Gamaliel the first, and a blasphemer and persecutor of The Way.

Shaul explained to the Galatians that after his dramatic revelation that Yeshua was the Messiah of Israel; he did not confer with those who were apostles before him but went off into the Arabian Desert. Alone in the desert, without anyone to explain his newfound faith, Shaul received a revelation of the gospel (Gal. 1:16). Shaul (from henceforth referred to as Paul) was adamant that he did not receive this gospel through the instruction of any human teacher, but he received it by direct revelation from Yeshua the Messiah. Further this revelation came with a specific call to take this gospel, received by revelation, to the Gentiles. This is important for us to remember when we read Paul's letters. He had received a message for the Gentiles with the revelatory authority of Yeshua the Messiah. In Romans 16:25, Paul describes this revelation as *my gospel.* He warned the Galatians that to reject the gospel as Paul had received it was to reject the truth of God (Gal. 1:6-9).

One could argue that at least among Christians, Paul's letters are the most popular books in the Bible. A survey of Sunday sermons across the wide spectrum of churches is likely to include a majority of messages based on Paul's writings. Paul's material is conducive to sermon material. He is logical and detailed and devotes most of his writing to topical explanations.

The irony is that despite the disproportionate focus on Pauline material, it seems that very little attention is given to Paul's unique role as the Apostle to the Gentiles. Paul's agitation with the Galatian Christians was not because he was anti-law but because the Galatians were rejecting the gospel to the Gentiles, specifically given to Paul by revelation on their behalf. When Paul wrote to the Romans that *the Gospel is the power of God unto salvation to everyone who believes, to the Jew first and also to the Greek*" (Rom. 1:16), he was making a statement that related to *his gospel,*" that is, the gospel he received by revelation to preach to the Gentiles. When Paul advised that some may consider a day holy and others, all days alike (Rom. 14:5), or some may have liberty to eat and some not (Rom. 14:2), he was not challenging the instructions of the Torah. Rather he was presenting the message as it was tailored for the Gentiles.

For Jewish believers there is no consideration of whether there are special days or all days are alike. The word to Jews is not; let each one be *"fully convinced in his own mind"* (Rom. 14:5). No Jew would ever take it upon his or her self to arbitrate which of Israel's holy days one should celebrate. The Scriptures assume all Jews, as a community would observe the feasts of HaShem.

Paul did not only receive a revelation. At the same time, he received a commission to take this revelation to the Gentiles. That the Gospel was even for the Gentiles was one of those truths the disciples at first could not bear. Yeshua himself had said, *"I was sent only to the lost sheep of the house of Israel"* (Matt. 15:24). No wonder when Yeshua told them to go into all the world, the disciples understood this to mean to go into all the world and preach the gospel to your Jewish brethren wherever they might live (see comment below on Acts 11:19).

It took a dramatic vision for Peter to consent to go with the Gentile representatives sent by Cornelius, the Roman centurion. The image of a sheet being lowered down from heaven containing all sorts of creatures, including reptiles, was not an image that would have stimulated Peter's already famished appetite. In response to the command to *"kill and eat"* (Acts 10:13), Peter raised the reasonable objection that as a Jew he had been faithful to observe the kosher laws set out in Leviticus 11.

Peter did not understand the message of the vision, but he knew it was not the abrogation of the kosher laws. After the vision repeated itself three times we read that Peter was "perplexed as to what the vision he had seen might mean" (Acts 10:17). Only after the Gentile delegation arrived, and after Peter received the assurance of the Holy Spirit to go with these three men does he understand that the vision related not to animal consumption but to the status of humanity before the Creator. Peter later explained, "God has shown me that I should not call any person common or unclean" (Acts 10:28).

However, this was all very difficult for Peter. Once he arrived at Cornelius' domicile the first words out of his mouth were, "You yourselves know how unlawful it is for a Jew to associate with or to visit any one of another nation" (Acts 10:28). Peter was out of his comfort zone, and just being in Cornelius' home pushed against everything he had heretofore understood about Jewish-Gentile relations.

To underscore the divine approval on this encounter, God poured out the Holy Spirit on these Gentiles, even before Peter could finish explaining the gospel to them. Acts records, "And the believers from among the circumcised who had come with Peter were amazed, because the gift of the Holy Spirit was poured out even on the Gentiles" (Acts 10:45).

They were amazed because it was inconceivable to their way of thinking that unclean Gentiles could become the recipients of God's Holy Spirit. Whether Peter and his Jewish companions could grasp it, or even whether they liked it or not, Gentiles were "made clean" by faith in Yeshua and now were included into the Body of Messiah. Folks that Peter had understood to be so defiled that he was violating scruples even to associate with them, were now filled with the same Holy Spirit that fell on the Jewish believers on the feast of Shavuot (Pentecost).

The pouring out of the Holy Spirit on Shavuot is regarded as the birth of the Church.[2] The common understanding is that as the disciples magnify God with "other tongues" the international character of the Church universal is displayed for all to hear. The assumption is that those "devout men from every nation under heaven" (Acts 2:5), were a representation of the nations, ordained to hear the witness of the gospel proclaimed to them in their own languages. This is only partly correct. This multi-national throng was not representatives from among the Gentiles. They were Jews from the diaspora obeying the command of the Torah to present themselves before HaShem in the place of God's choosing during the three pilgrim feasts.

Shavuot is the second of these feasts that require Jews from wherever they live to assemble at the Temple.[3] As Luke records, "Now there were dwelling in Jerusalem Jews, devout men from every nation under heaven" (Acts 2:5). Acts 2:11

---

[2] The word "Church" evokes many dimensions of meaning. Within the Apostolic Writings the word is ἐκκλησίᾳ (ekklesia, assembly), and this corresponds to the Hebrew word קָהֵל (kahal, assembly, i.e. "Moses spoke the words of this song…in the ears of all the assembly (קָהָל) of Israel" (Deut. 31:30). The word Church has come to mean a new assembly of God's people standing apart from God's people Israel. Though one can speak of Israel without referring to the Church I do not believe it is correct to see the Church opposite Israel. Rather, the church is comprised of both Jews (Israel) and Gentiles (the nations) joined together as One New Man by faith in Israel's Messiah. I will use the term church to mean the assembly of those in Messiah.

[3] The other pilgrim feasts are Unleavened Bread and Sukkot. (Exod. 23:14-17; Deut. 16:16)

adds that there were proselytes included in this international gathering, but the emphasis is that this is a gathering of Israel, not the nations. Peter's address to the crowd begins, "Men of Judea and all who dwell in Jerusalem ... Men of Israel, hear these words." Peter concludes his message, "Let all the house of Israel therefore know for certain that God has made him (Yeshua) both Lord and Christ" (Acts 2:14, 22, and 36). Acts 2 is a fulfillment of God's promise to Israel. The witness of the apostles is to the "men of Israel."

The Holy Spirit was poured out on Israel as the fulfillment of the God of Israel's covenant pledge to His people. The Hebrew Scriptures anticipate God pouring out His Holy Spirit on Israel (Isa. 59:21; Ezek. 36:27; 37:14; 39:29). The outpouring of the Holy Spirit in Acts 2 is not a reconstitution of the people of God into an international company; rather it is the promise of Israel's regeneration and spiritual transformation first anticipated in the Torah.

Deuteronomy 30:6 declares that Israel's return from exile will include a spiritual transformation, "And the LORD your God will circumcise your heart and the heart of your offspring, so that you will love the LORD your God with all your heart and with all your soul, that you may live" (Deut. 30:6). When we understand Acts 2 to be a Jewish event based on the Torah and the Prophetic Writings then it underscores the radical impact of Cornelius the Gentile also being filled with the Holy Spirit.

Israel is a small country and word traveled fast. When Peter arrived back in Jerusalem the brethren were waiting for him. They were not waiting to rejoice with Peter over the marvellous extension of grace towards Cornelius the Gentile.

30

They were waiting to hold Peter to account for stepping beyond their perceived boundaries towards their Gentile neighbours – "You went to uncircumcised men and ate with them" (Acts 11:3).

I can almost see Peter backing up and submissively raising his hands in a defensive posture, "Wait a minute brothers; honestly, it was not my idea." Peter then recalled the whole story explaining the shocking three-fold vision of unclean animals being lowered down from the heavens coinciding with three Gentiles arriving at the door. He was instructed by the Holy Spirit to go with them, and when he arrived at their master's house, just as he began to speak, "The Holy Spirit fell on them [Gentiles] just as on us [Jews] at the beginning" (Acts 11:15). Peter was quick to emphasize, "Who was I to stand in God's way?" (Acts 11:15-17).

The response of Peter's accusers is telling of just how dramatic this encounter with Gentiles was for the Messianic community in Jerusalem. Verse 18 reads, "When they heard these things they fell silent." They needed a moment to sort this incredible tale out; Peter's encounter with Cornelius and his household fell way outside their theological grid. I think we often miss this. We are so comfortable with the name Jesus Christ that we forget "Christ" is a totally Jewish term – the expected and anointed King of Israel who would rule over his people Israel from Jerusalem. The prophets speak of a universal dimension to Messiah's rule, but to a first century Jew, the Gentiles coming into the kingdom would be understood to come after Messiah's glorious revelation to all Israel.

Their silent pause allowed room for a dramatic shift in their understanding. The "light bulb" went on (I am sure accompanied by a loud "ding" that everyone heard), "and they glorified God, saying, 'then to the Gentiles also God has granted repentance that leads to life'" (Acts 11:18). What a radical idea! The Gentiles were included in God's salvation plan. Praise God that those first Jewish disciples had enough grace and humility to receive this good news. Salvation in Yeshua was not only for Israel but also for all nations.

Following the church in Jerusalem's acceptance of the Gentiles inclusion in the "repentance that leads to life," the narrative in Acts shifts to a report on Jewish witness in the diaspora. Jewish evangelists were preaching the gospel "as far as Phoenicia and Cyprus and Antioch" (Acts 11:19). Following the accepted practice of the pre-Peter/Cornelius encounter, they preached "to no one except Jews" (Acts 11:19b). I think it is doubtful that these Jewish evangelists were privy to the recent events surrounding Peter and Cornelius, and yet we read that shortly after the Jerusalem church came to understand that the gospel is also for Gentiles, some of these Jewish evangelists who had limited their message to fellow Jews now started preaching to "the Hellenists" (Acts11:20).

Hellenists can mean Greek speaking Jews (Acts 6:1; 9:29), but here the context indicates these are Greek speaking Gentiles. The Church, on account of Jerusalem's coming into line with God's purposes for Jews and Gentiles together in Messiah, shifted the spiritual atmosphere and opened a new liberty for evangelists in the diaspora to reach out for the first time to Gentiles.

The result is that many Gentiles accept the gospel. Contrary to popular view, it is Acts 11 not Acts 2 that represents the birth of the church among the nations. Jerusalem gets word of this, but now instead of upbraiding these Jewish evangelists for preaching to Gentiles (like they had done with Peter), they sent Barnabas as their emissary to support and encourage these new Gentile believers. The grace of God was with Barnabas and "a great many people were added to the Lord" (Acts 11:24). Barnabas had previously met Paul (Acts 9:27), and had stood as Paul's advocate before the Apostles in Jerusalem. Now he was responsible for discipling a new community of Gentile believers, and he knew the right man for the job – Shaul of Tarsus (Paul), the man the Holy Spirit had commissioned to be the Apostle to the Gentiles.

How ironic that of all Jews chosen to preach this salvation to the Gentiles, God would choose a Jew who had been so radically zealous for the traditions of his fathers. If you think it was a big deal for the Galilean fisherman Peter to go to a Gentile's home, what was it like for the Pharisee Shaul of Tarsus? Yet, Paul had been chosen to take the Gospel to the Gentiles, and he needed a direct revelation from the Holy Spirit to ensure the message was transmitted without any human interference or prejudice, according to the will and plan of Heaven.

But despite the Peter/Cornelius encounter, the establishment of a new Gentile based congregation in Antioch, and Barnabas and Paul's subsequent success preaching the gospel to Gentiles in Cyprus and Asia (Acts 13-14), not everyone in the Messianic Jewish community was convinced that Gentiles should be accepted as members of God's household. Another Jewish delegation reached Antioch, this time informing the believers that the Gentiles were required to undergo circumcision to enter the family of God: *"But some men came down from Judea and were teaching the brothers, 'Unless you are circumcised according to the custom of Moses, you cannot be saved"* (Acts 15:1).

This was not just a matter of physical appearance. These Jewish believers expected the Gentiles to join the household of Israel by converting to Judaism. Circumcision is the outward sign of the covenant between God and Israel. To undergo circumcision is to join the Jewish nation as Jews. For those who were demanding that the Gentiles required circumcision it was not sufficient for Gentiles to enter the family as Gentiles. Along with faith in Messiah and turning away from sin, there also needed to be a shift from Gentile to Jewish identity.

Before we come down too hard on these "Judaizers," we should recall that they had good precedent for expecting Gentiles to accept circumcision and join the nation of Israel. When Israel departed Egypt a throng of Gentiles joined them in their exodus (Exod.12:38). Some of these folks had a difficult time conforming to the God of Israel's expectations (see, Lev. 24:10-12; Num. 11:4), but they were welcomed as full status citizens in Israel. They achieved this status by entering the family through embracing Israel's covenant status and Israeli identity.[4] The outpouring of the Holy Spirit on Gentiles prior to their entrance into Israel as circumcised converts indicated a new way for Gentile inclusion into the family of God.

---

[4] Caleb the son of Jephunneh represented the tribe of Judah as one of the 12 sent out to spy the land of Canaan. Numbers 32:12 states Caleb was a Kennizite. There is some indication that Caleb was a Gentile from the mixed multitude (See, Gen. 15:19).

Barnabas and Paul, who had witnessed the Holy Spirit at work among the Gentiles, head up a delegation sent to Jerusalem to seek the Apostle's directive on this matter. Seeking the advice of centralized religious authorities is a long held Jewish custom that continues on in Rabbinic Judaism to this day.[5] Paul and Barnabas detailed how the Holy Spirit had moved among Gentiles in the empire. Some within the Jerusalem congregation (believers from within the Pharisee tradition) are still not convinced, insisting that Gentiles be circumcised "and keep the Law of Moses" (Acts 15:5). That is, they contended that the Gentile believers must cease to remain Gentiles and join Messiah as converts to the Jewish nation.

Ironically, the chief defenders of the Gentiles are the two foremost apostles to the Jewish people, Shimon Kefa (Peter) and Yakov ben Yoseph (James, the Lord's brother). Peter begins by rehearsing his encounter with Cornelius; again pointing out that Cornelius and his household received the Holy Spirit as uncircumcised Gentiles. Paul and Barnabas back Peter by recounting the miraculous signs and wonders the Holy Spirit had performed through their ministry among the Gentiles. Now Yakov summarizes the matter in order to give a ruling on the dispute:

---

[5] The practice is known as Responsa: Letters presented in the form of questions sent to the central religious authorities to elicit formal "responses" that would determine the rule for community practice. The council in Jerusalem (Acts 15) does not comply with the genre of responsa literature, as the dispute is not set out as a formal written question. But it does follow certain features similar to responsa. Like responsa literature an outlying community is seeking a formal response from the central religious authorities (the Apostles and Elders in Jerusalem). Like responsa literature the decision is formalized in writing and sent back to the inquiring community.

"Brothers, listen to me. Simeon has related how God first visited the Gentiles, to take from them a people for his name. And with this the words of the prophets agree, just as it is written, 'After this I will return, and I will rebuild the tent of David that has fallen; I will rebuild its ruins, and I will restore it, that the remnant of mankind may seek the Lord, and all the Gentiles who are called by my name,' says the Lord, who makes these things known from of old." (Acts 15:13–18)

Yakov's ruling captures two essential dimensions of One New Man. First, this was not a new shift in God's plan; it had always been God's intention to include the nations in His family. What Peter experienced in Caesarea with Cornelius the Italian was in agreement with God's revelation contained in the prophetic writings. Second, God's intention for the nations was that they join the family as the nations. They were to be a people "for His name." If the Gentiles were to be circumcised (become Jews), they would no longer bear witness as a people for God's name among the nations. Gentile identity is important to the plan. If Gentiles become Jews they do not fulfill their call to bear witness as a people for God's name from among the Gentiles.

The Gentiles cannot fulfill the prophetic expectation to be a people for God's name if they no longer bear Gentile identity. This is the central rationale for Yakov's decision. The group that demanded Gentile circumcision did not embrace the plan of God revealed in the prophetic writings. Therefore, Yakov, the apostles, and the elders in Jerusalem present a formal written answer to the Gentile believers affirming their identity as Gentiles, only requiring four prohibitions:

1. Abstain from eating food sacrificed to idols
2. Abstain from sexual immorality
3. Abstain from eating blood
4. Abstain from meat slaughtered by strangulation

This list reflects a submission to Torah that maintains Gentile identity. It certainly is not a *carte blanche* exemption from the law of God to murder, steal, and lie just as long as one does not eat blood. However, it exempts the Gentiles from those commands in the Torah that touch on Jewish distinctiveness – that is, circumcision, kosher laws, feast days, agricultural, social, economic, and cultic commandments particular to Israel.[6]

Yakov's four restrictions corresponded to four restrictions imposed on the native Israeli and the "stranger" (Gentile) among them as set out in Leviticus 17 and 18. That is, both the native Israeli and the Gentile among them were to abstain from blood (Lev. 17:10), must only offer sacrifice at the

---

[6] In Romans 14:1-5 Paul outlines a liberty based on personal conscience with respect to celebration of holy days and food restrictions. This is in keeping with the Acts 15 decision for Gentiles. Jews do not have the liberty to decide whether they will determine by conscience to observe a day determined as holy by Torah. Likewise, Jews do not have the liberty to decide for themselves to eat or not to eat foods outside the restrictions of Leviticus 11. Paul would never encourage Jews to make independent decisions on these matters specifically commanded in Torah. Like all the Messianic Jews of his day, Paul observed the commandments of Torah (Acts 21:24).

tabernacle so as to abstain from idolatry (Lev. 17:7-8, see also Lev. 18:21), must slaughter animals by cutting the animals throat (precluding strangulation, see Lev. 17:13), and must abstain from sexual immorality (Lev. 18:1-26).[7]

When all the leaders agreed that this was the Holy Spirit's determination for Gentile believers, they drafted the decision in a letter and sent it by the hands of a chosen delegation to accompany Paul and Barnabas back to Antioch. As the apostle to the Gentiles it was fitting that Paul would take the lead role in disseminating the leader's ruling for Gentile practice within the Messianic community. Paul is a champion of Gentile liberty. Too often Paul has been portrayed as rejecting Torah, but this is a misunderstanding of Paul's ministry and his specific call. Paul was not anti-Torah. However, he was militantly against the movement within the Messianic Jewish community that did not recognize God's plan to have a people from among the Gentiles for His name.

Those Messianic Jewish evangelists who ignored the Council's decision and sought to convert Gentiles so as to forsake their Gentile identity were not only disobedient to the leaders of the Messianic Jewish community, they were at cross purposes with the man God had appointed as the apostle to the Gentiles.[8] In a Jewish evangelism context, they could have

---

[7] In most years, the Haftorah (supplemental scripture) portion to coincide with Leviticus 17-18 includes Amos 9. Perhaps Yakov may have put these scriptures together on account of their formal connection in the Parashot (weekly Torah portion) readings. Currently, this is the Ashkenazi tradition. Conceivably, it may extend back to the first century, but Acts 15 is the only witness to that connection. [See, Mark S. Kinzer, "Post Missionary Messianic Judaism" (Grand Rapids: Brazos Press, 2005), 160.]

[8] In context, the controversy in Galatia likely occurred before the Council of Acts 15, but those who preached that Gentiles must be circumcised

been advocates of the gospel. In a Gentile context, they were enemies of the gospel – at least the gospel to the Gentiles that Paul received by revelation. Paul's letter to the Galatians burns with passionate anger against those who would seek to persuade Gentiles to become Jews.

This is not because Paul was anti-Semitic or had renounced his own Jewish identity. On the contrary, it is because he knew by revelation that the salvation of his people and the great purposes of God depended on the Gentiles being a people for God's name as Gentiles. *[NOT CONVERTS TO JUDAISM]*

Paul's ministry among the Gentiles was motivated by his passion for his own people. He suffered more hardships, more misunderstandings, more betrayals, and more violence against his person.[9] He worked harder than any of the other apostles.[10] All along he burned with an "unceasing anguish" in his heart, even to the point of willing to accept eternal damnation for the sake of "his kinsmen according to the flesh" (Rom.9:1-3).[11]

At the end of the Book of Acts, at the end of Luke's chronicle of Paul's journeys preaching the gospel among the Gentiles, Paul gave this testimony – "It is because of the hope of Israel that I am wearing this chain" (Acts 28:20). Everything Paul did, he did for the sake of "the hope of Israel." Without the Gentiles as a people for God's name, Israel's hope

---

continued their message after the council decision (See, Phil. 3:2; 2 Cor. 11:1-33).

[9] Paul's list of hardships in 2 Corinthians 11:23-33 details the incredible price he was willing to pay to fulfill his calling.

[10] 1 Cor. 15:10

[11] Paul's yearning for his kinsman was not ethnic sentimentality. He testified that his conscience bore witness in the Holy Spirit. The anguish he felt was the same willingness to suffer for the sake of others exemplified by Messiah Yeshua.

would never come to fruition. No wonder Paul was so angry with those who encouraged the Gentile believers in Galatia to reject the Council decision and seek to enter the family of God by way of circumcision. The Gentiles were a key to Israel's salvation. Paul knew this and therefore gave everything he had to see the Gentiles come to faith in Messiah.

With respect to Jewish disciples, Paul demonstrated adherence to Torah by his own conviction and practice.[12] In Acts 21, Yakov informs Paul that rumours were spreading throughout the Messianic community that Paul was teaching, "to forsake Moses" (Acts 21:21). In order to squelch these false rumours, Yakov requested that Paul demonstrate his adherence to Torah by joining four believers who have taken a Nazarite vow – not only paying for their Temple sacrifice, but joining in their purification ceremony himself.

Yakov's intent is that by Paul doing so "all will know that there is nothing in what they have been told about you, but that you yourself also live in observance of the law" (Acts 21:24). Paul was being asked to make a public declaration of his own convictions. This is not simply "being a Jew to the Jew." Yakov assumed Paul observed Torah and was not teaching that Jews should forsake Moses. By participating in a Temple rite, Paul was in effect validating Yakov's assumption. To be simply accommodating Yakov and the

---

[12] See, David Rudolph, "Messianic Judaism in Antiquity and in the Modern Era" in *Introduction to Messianic Judaism*, editors, David Rudolph and Joel Willitts (Grand Rapids: Zondervan, 2013) 22-24.

believers who were "zealous for the law" (Acts 21:20), would have been disingenuous, even hypocritical.[13]

In Acts 15, Yakov had noted that the prophets testify of God's intention to take a people from among the Gentiles for His name. Later, in his letter to the Romans, Paul delivered a benediction that also testified that God's plan for the Gentiles was contained in the prophetic writings:

> *"Now to him who is able to strengthen you according to my gospel and the preaching of Jesus Christ, according to the revelation of the mystery that was kept secret for long ages but has now been disclosed and through the prophetic writings has been made known to all nations, according to the command of the eternal God, to bring about the obedience of faith."* (Rom. 16:25–26)

The gospel Paul names as "his gospel" had been made known "through the prophetic writings." By extension, this same gospel revealed in the prophetic writings is also revealed in the Torah because the prophetic writings are all based on Torah. Paul says as much to the Galatians:

> *"And the Scripture, foreseeing that God would justify the Gentiles by faith, preached the gospel beforehand to Abraham, saying, 'In you shall all the nations be blessed.'"* (Gal. 3:8)

---

[13] I am indebted to Dr. David Rudolph, a former professor, for my understanding of Acts 21.

I will have much more to say about this mystery now revealed, but for now, I would point out that the gospel Paul received by revelation in Arabia was this mystery now revealed, and this mystery is foremost a message to the Gentiles. Please understand, I am *not* saying the Gospel is only for Gentiles and not for Jews – may it never be! God forbid I should say that. What I am saying is that the mystery revealed to Paul by revelation is the message he presented to the Gentiles.

There was a mystery that they needed to know, and God had chosen Paul as the herald of this good news. Paul was the key messenger to present the gospel to all nations. The intent of this plan was to bring all nations into obedience to the faith (Rom. 16:27). Both Yakov and Paul say that this plan for the nations is revealed in the prophetic scriptures. We will address the "mystery now revealed" on our section on Ephesians. It is noteworthy that the plan of God for the nations was always the plan from the beginning – even though through Paul the mystery "kept secret" in past times was now revealed.

This mystery was hidden in plain sight. It is not new in the sense that there was never any indication of God's plan for the Gentiles prior to the Apostolic Writings. It is new in the sense that despite the witness of the Tanakh, it was only through the revelation of the Gospel that Paul received in the desert that the plan for Gentile inclusion within the people of God was fully articulated.

Some theologians regard the Church as a complete mystery without reference in the Tanakh. The classic dispensationalist view understands the Church to be "'an intercalation,' meaning an insertion of a period of time into a previously planned schedule or calendar of events." [14] The Church is a sort of historical interruption in God's plan for Israel that is subsequently removed from history (by the rapture). At that juncture, God continues His plans and promises to Israel that is ultimately expressed in the Millennium.

This is not a book on the last days, so I will not go into detail on those specific matters. What is important for our purposes is to see that God's people in the nations and God's people Israel were always intended in the plan of God to be one in Messiah. The mystery of the church is not any sort of parenthetical plan, it has always been the plan – hidden, but hidden in plain sight within the prophetic writings.

The goal is to bring about *"obedience of faith"* for both Jew and Gentile. At the heart of obedience, is the command to love one another. Obedience is ultimately about love, and love exists only within relationship. Our relationship with God creates a relationship with one another. We cannot come to the place of obedience without recognizing our relationship together as Jew and Gentile in Messiah.

Paul is very cognizant of the potential pitfalls should we fail to recognize our relationship together as One New Man. Paul's gospel contained warnings to the Gentiles – not to boast against the Jewish branches that had been broken off for unbelief (Rom. 11:18), and to not be ignorant of the mystery of Israel lest the Gentiles become conceited (Rom. 11:25). We read in Acts 11 that those first Jewish believers were in danger

[14] Wayne Grudem. "Grudem's Systematic Theology" electronic edition, Whitefish, MN: Bits and Bytes, 2008) 872. Grudem is referencing Lewis Sperry Chafer's classic dispensationalist theology, "Systematic Theology."

of the same sort of arrogance against the Gentiles and needed a dramatic sign from the Holy Spirit to get them on track with God's purposes, not only for themselves the Jewish people, but for the Gentiles as well.

Regrettably, today, we have the opposite situation. The Gentile church has failed to understand the mystery of Israel. The result has been a boasting against the branches that Paul had warned about. Just as those first Jewish believers required a dramatic shift in their understanding to recognize God's purposes for Jew and Gentile together, so too the Gentile church is now faced with making the same sort of shift away from Gentile exclusivity to expand their call on behalf of Israel and the Jewish people. Paul wrote extensively about this; and indeed, that is what this book is all about.

Even as I, a Jew had to disentangle myself from the blinding effects of replacement theology, the whole Body of Messiah is faced with the challenge of extricating itself from the arrogance produced by failing to understand the mystery. Now is the time for the Gentiles to make the same sort of shift that the early Jews made back in Acts 11. When the light came on for those early Jewish believers, they glorified God. Their view of His plan had been expanded to see the greater majesty of Yeshua's salvation extending beyond Israel to the nations. May the Church in the nations now give glory to God as their vision is expanded to see Yeshua's salvation ultimately fulfilling all of God's promises to Israel, the apple of His eye.

Response: The Revelation of the Mystery
Dean Bye, Director, Return Ministries

Dean adds a further explanation of the gospel Paul received by revelation based on the doxology of Romans 16:25-27. (MS)

"Now to him who is able to strengthen you according to my gospel and the preaching of Jesus Christ, according to the revelation of the mystery." (Rom. 16:25)

One could think that Paul, the apostle to the Gentiles, had major chutzpah to sign off his epistle by exhorting the Romans to be strengthened by 'his' gospel. Paul was not boasting, he was acknowledging that his gospel was the gospel of Jesus Christ received by revelation of the mystery. This is the gospel message not only for the Romans of the first century but now, for Christians living in the 21st century. This is a gospel connected to the people of Israel and the prophetic writings. Therefore, this is a gospel also connected to the land of Israel.

Paul explained that his gospel was according to the "revelation of the mystery" revealed through the prophetic writings. The importance of the prophetic writings to the disciple of Christ in this generation cannot be understated. Prophetic words speak to the prophetic times in which we live and provide the prophetic instruction on how to act in these times.

I was taught that the preaching of Jesus Christ was an integral part of every Christian life. I've since learned, that the apostolic witness preached Jesus Christ according to the revelation of the mystery that was hidden for ages past (Rom16:25). A major turning point in my Christian journey began when I started to study the prophetic writings in light of prophetic fulfillments actually happening in my lifetime.

Unique to our generation is the fulfillment of the prophetic scriptures promise of Israel being restored back to their own land. Whatever theology you hold to, no one can dispute that the prophetic scriptures anticipate Israel returning to the land from the four corners of the earth and the reality of the Jewish people returning from those four corners to the land of Israel in our lifetime. This perspective on the prophetic writings has challenged me in every area of my life. I've come to understand that as a disciple of Jesus Christ, I have a responsibility to obey the prophetic scriptures as led by the Holy Spirit. I have never been the same since. Praise the Lord!

Turn On! Get Fully Engaged! (With all 3 Prongs)

You might have access to the power but you have to be fully plugged in to be properly engaged and effectively turned on. I'm reminded of a Sunday morning service in a church where I was scheduled to speak; the worship team was fussing around to get sound out of their equipment and through the sound system. The soundboard was plugged in and all its lights were on, but no sound was getting through the equipment. The soundman was late so you can imagine the anxiety just prior to the service. When the soundman finally arrived, he simply pushed the large electrical plug further into the wall ensuring that all 3 prongs were securely fastened. Now the sound system was fully engaged with all 3 prongs properly making contact. The necessary power was effectively flowing through the system, providing the amplification that matched the lights on the soundboard.

It seems as Christians, we can sometimes think we're plugged in properly, and to others it may even look like the lights are on, however we may lack the fullness of God's power flowing through us. To be truly strengthened according to the gospel, we need to ensure that we're fully engaged and turned on.

In closing the letter to the Roman church, Paul praises God Almighty with these words:

> *"Now to him who is able to strengthen you **according** to my gospel and the preaching of Jesus Christ, **according** to the revelation of the mystery that was kept secret for long ages but has now been disclosed and through the prophetic writings has been made known to all nations, **according** to the command of the eternal God, to bring about the obedience of faith—to the only wise God be glory forevermore through Jesus Christ! Amen."* (Rom. 16:25–27)

Paul is worshipping the only wise God and at the same time instructing us that God's power is available to us as long as we are fully plugged into the power source. Paul was very intentional to 'insert' three significant points (the three prongs of the plug) to ensure we connect to God's power source.

In these closing words he included three phrases each beginning with the preposition 'according to.' By repeating the phrase 'according to' three times, Paul harmonized three key points to his main thought.

When we are correctly 'plugged into' these three key points we receive the power of God to be strengthened according to Paul's gospel. This empowering is the Holy Spirit's strength to ultimately bring us *to the obedience of faith.* Let us look at each of these 'accordings' set out in the doxology of Romans 16:25-27.

#1 *According to my gospel and the preaching of Jesus Christ*

Paul closes his gospel with a doxology that is intended to conclude in a few words all that he has just written. He tells the reader that God is able to strengthen his faith if first they accept the gospel of Christ that Paul had explained in detail in the body of his letter. He calls this gospel his own. He may as well have said, "This is Christ's story and I'm sticking to it and so should you!" However, Paul's gospel and preaching of Christ needs to be understood also according to the revelation of the mystery.

#2 *According to the revelation of the mystery*

How are we supposed to preach Jesus Christ? Does the Lord have a specific strategy that works? The Apostle Paul stressed that the preaching of Jesus Christ is of prime importance. But this preaching must be according to the revelation of the mystery. A mystery Paul explained, that was hidden for ages past but now has been made known by the prophetic scriptures. In Romans 11, Paul gave a stern warning to the church not to be ignorant of this mystery; otherwise it would lead to pride. Paul explained that according to this mystery, Israel had been blinded until the Gentiles come into their fullness.

> *"For I do not desire, brethren, that you should be ignorant of this mystery, lest you should be wise in your own opinion, that blindness in part has happened to Israel until the fullness of the Gentiles has come in."*
> (Rom. 11:25 NKJV)

The word 'fullness' could be understood as completeness or maturity.[15] The Gentiles' maturity or fullness is a vital part in God's plan of redemption. Paul knew this and realized that the salvation of his people depended on the Gentiles coming into the commonwealth of Israel with a maturity that understood and acted upon the revelation of the mystery. The apostle to the Gentiles understood the vital role Gentiles were to play in the purposes of God but also the danger the church faced should the Gentiles remain ignorant of the revelation of the mystery.

---

[15] The concept of "Fullness of the Gentiles" is discussed in greater detail in Chapter 5

Paul had taught in Romans 11, that the Gentiles were the engrafted parts of the olive tree. They needed to be wary of losing sight of their roots. Otherwise, it could lead to pride. Instead of moving towards softening the hardness of Israel, the Gentile church would then become hard themselves, further entrenching Israel in her own hardness. Sadly, our Christian history records that this is exactly what happened. Thankfully, we live in the time when many Gentile Christians are recognizing their own hardness which has been brought on by their ignorance of the mystery. Thank God for His mercy, as many in the Gentile church have been making an unprecedented move of repentance in regards to our sad history with the people and land of Israel.

Paul explained the mystery to the church in Ephesus this way:

> *"And the mystery is this: Because of Christ Jesus, the good news has given the Gentiles a share in the promises that God gave to the Jews. God has also let the Gentiles be part of the same body."* (Eph. 3:6 CEV)

It was good news that by God's grace, the Gentiles shared in God's promises for the Jewish people, and were welcomed into the family of God. As non-Jews, we Gentiles were added to the family. There was never any intention for us to replace the original, or older children and heirs. What perhaps has confused many Gentiles in the church is that not long after God made a way for the Gentiles to be added to His family through Jesus Christ, some of the older children (Jews) were sent out of the house because they did not keep to the original house rules.

In Romans 11, Paul uses the analogy of natural branches broken off - this should not be understood to mean the Gentile church replaced Israel. What's more, the Father's expectations of the newer members of the family (Gentiles), seemed rather relaxed, giving time for these adopted children to grow into maturity. Yes, the younger children have it so much easier until they reach an age when they can take on greater responsibility. The Father's greatest expectation was that His new members (Gentiles) would follow His sinless Son, and learn from His example as an elder brother.

In our Father's great mercy and wisdom, once the younger children would attain to greater maturity or fullness, Jesus would lead them to be part of the solution in uniting the whole family, Jew and Gentile to the Father and His ways. It would begin with the younger children understanding the family plan, then attracting the older children back to Daddy's house and land. Ultimately, these younger children were to comfort the older children with boundless love and mercy, so that they (the Jewish people) might have a change of heart towards Jesus, the head of God's household. Furthermore, the Father in such amazing wisdom would then use His older children, now again reunited with the younger children, to attract many more Gentiles into the family. This united family, now with the addition of many more members representing every nation, would share in the promises together!

Where was this *"revelation of the mystery"* found? The apostle Paul explained that the *"revelation of the mystery"* was kept secret for many generations (Rom. 16:25; Col. 1:26; Eph. 3:9).

The family plan was for a set time. However, he told us plainly that the revelation is contained in the prophetic writings (Rom. 16:26). When the Gentiles obey Paul's gospel they will fulfill the prophetic writings that speak in many places about the nations worshipping the God of Israel and uniting with the people of Israel. Paul's gospel of Christ, preached in harmony with this mystery, revealed through the prophetic scriptures, is the key for his own people's revival. Subsequently, Israel's revival would lead to the salvation of many more in the nations to obedient faith.

#3 *According to the command of the eternal God*

Paul was insistent that his gospel preached Jesus Christ in accordance to the revelation of this mystery, disclosed through the prophetic writings. However, he wanted his readers to know that all this was according to the command of the eternal God. This was God's command to those who had the revelation of the mystery. When Paul wrote about the mystery to the church in Ephesus, he declared that the mystery of the Gentiles being fellow heirs with Israel *"was according to the eternal purpose that he has realized in Christ Jesus our Lord"* (Eph. 3:11). This plan of Jew and Gentile together was God's plan from the beginning.

Why was Paul so adamant about encouraging a distinct order regarding the gospel he preached? When we discover God's order we have an easier time giving up our own methods and switching to God's methods. God's plan is ultimately about all nations coming to the obedience of the faith. It is about worldwide revival. We all want to see that great revival of all nations coming to the obedience of faith.

According to Romans 16:25-27, the power for revival is released when we 'plug into' Paul's three prong approach: 1. We follow the gospel of Jesus Christ that Paul preached, a gospel connected to the Jewish people. 2. The gospel is according to the revelation of the mystery. This is the mystery set out in the prophetic writings that anticipate Israel's restoration and the salvation of the Gentiles. 3. Ultimately, God's plan for Israel and the Church is so that all nations come to the obedience of faith.

CHAPTER 2

The Mystery of One New Man in the Hebrew Scriptures

Dean Bye explained that in Romans 16:25,26 Paul described the gospel he preached as "my gospel," and attributed it to the revelation he received, a mystery now made known and disclosed *"through the prophetic writings."* As I had explained earlier, this is the gospel as Paul received it by revelation in the Arabian Desert (Gal. 1:11-17). However, in order to bring some clarification, Paul added that this mystery is revealed *"through the prophetic writings [which] has been made known to all nations"* (Rom. 16:26). The mystery that was hidden was hidden in plain sight within the Hebrew Scriptures. Even in his letter to the Galatians, where Paul is emphatic that he is carrying a special revelation on behalf of the Gentiles that no man taught him, Paul recognized that this "new" revelation is not new in a way that it is apart or contrary to what had been revealed in the Hebrew Scriptures.

Perhaps some understand God's purposes to make in Messiah "One New Man" as a new revelation, first revealed in Ephesians 2. I would counter that One New Man has been God's plan all along and is alluded to many times in the

rew Scriptures. The plan of HaShem is contained in the
...rew Scriptures. It is a mistake to understand the "New
Testament" as something completely new, in the sense that it
is apart from what came before.

A better way to understand the 'newness' of the New
Covenant is to see Yeshua's ministry, including his death,
burial and resurrection as the expansion of the purposes of
HaShem in and through Israel as recorded in the Hebrew
Scriptures. The New Covenant is not out of keeping with all
the other covenants HaShem made with Israel. The New
Covenant (made with Israel and Judah, Jer. 31:31) is
anticipated in the all the Hebrew Scriptures. Yeshua upbraided
the disciples on the road to Emmaus because they were "slow
in heart to understand all that the prophets had spoken"
(Luke 24:25). If they had understood the prophetic writings
they would have understood that Messiah had to suffer to enter
into his glory (Luke 24:26).

Paul explained to the Galatians, *"The Scripture, foreseeing
that God would justify the Gentiles by faith, preached the gospel
beforehand to Abraham, saying, 'In you shall all the nations be
blessed'"* (Gal. 3:8, quoting Gen. 12:3). Even the Torah
(Genesis), preaches the gospel -- to the Gentiles. This is not
really so surprising, many Christian preachers have quoted the
old maxim, "The Old Testament is the New Testament
concealed, and the New Testament is the Old Testament
revealed."

In a sense, this is true, but it exposes an error that has
dogged the church's growth towards maturity ever since the
early Church Fathers determined that the church among the
Gentiles had replaced Israel as the chosen people.

If we understand the Hebrews scriptures only as a co concealing HaShem's plan of salvation in Yeshua, then HaShem's relationship with Israel becomes a backdrop to the real story. Israel is a sort of set decoration used by the heavenly director as the background for the message of Messiah. Once Messiah appears, the purpose for the set decoration has ended, or at least it fades out into insignificance. But, if we acknowledge the scripture's affirmation that the New Covenant is made with "the house of Israel and the house of Judah," then Israel is not a backdrop but the main player in the drama. Israel never recedes into the background. After all, Yeshua is the Messiah, David's greater son who rules *"over the house of Jacob forever"* (Luke 1:33).

Israel is always in focus in the scriptures. However, it is also incorrect to see HaShem's dealings with the Gentiles as a new and unexpected development. The Gentiles were not out of focus before the New Covenant. The Gentiles were always in focus because HaShem's choosing of Israel was from the outset for the purpose of Israel and the nations joined together in mutual blessing: One New Man.

The Gospel's ultimate purpose is to gather all things both in heaven and on earth in Messiah (Eph. 1:9,10). As Paul also noted in Ephesians, this plan as it relates to both Jews and Gentiles (those who are gathered together on earth) has been HaShem's plan from the very beginning. We have been chosen in Messiah *"before the foundation of the world"* (Eph. 1:4).

The "gospel preached to Abraham" that Paul described to the Galatians contains the promise; *"I will bless those who bless you, and I will curse him who curses you"* (Gen. 12:3).

I used to think this was evidence of how much HaShem loved Abraham, "If you are good to the one I love, I will be good to you, if you are bad…watch out!"

I have since revised my understanding of this reciprocal formula in Genesis 12:3. The promise of blessing or curse is not so much a reflection on Abraham's favoured position, but as the potential for blessing upon the ones who connect into Abraham's blessed status. Those who recognize Abraham as the one blessed by HaShem, bless Abraham so as to demonstrate their love for the One who established Abraham to be chosen for blessing. In return, the same One who blessed Abraham blesses these ones as well. <u>This is One New Man: the Gentiles bless the father of the Jewish people and they are blessed in return</u>[16].

This is the pattern HaShem had determined in His choice of the Jewish people. He chose them as His *"treasured possession among all peoples"* (Exod. 19:5). The Almighty has every right to do this because as the creator, He has all authority over His creation, as He explained to Israel, I chose you, *"for all the earth is mine"* (Exod. 19:5b). But this choosing goes far beyond the entitlements of the Chooser. HaShem goes on to explain the purpose of this choosing in the next verse: *"and you shall be to me a kingdom of priests and a holy nation"* (Exod. 19:6).

A priest functions as an intermediary, an intercessor who stands between God and the people to represent the people to God and God to the people. Speaking of Yeshua's eternal

---

[16] This is not to discount Paul's argument in Romans 4:9-12 that the righteousness Abraham receives by faith occurs before his circumcision so as to make Abraham "the father of all who believe" (Rom. 4:11), whether they be circumcised or uncircumcised. In this context I am focusing on Abraham as the father of the circumcised.

priesthood, the Writer of Hebrews notes, *"Consequently* [*One New Man*] *able to save to the uttermost those who draw near to God* [*him, since he always lives to make intercession for them"* (Heb. 7:25).

Aaron and his sons were appointed by HaShem to be priests on Israel's behalf. Several times the Torah records that when Israel sinned Aaron (and Moses) made intercession for the nation (e.g. Num. 14:5; 16:22; 20:6). Israel had priests on their behalf, but Exodus 19:6 declares that the whole nation was to function as priests. If Aaron and his sons were appointed priests on Israel's behalf, then for whom does the nation of Israel function as priests? The answer is that Israel, the kingdom of priests, functions as priests on behalf of all the other nations of the world.

From the start, HaShem's plan was for Israel and the nations to be joined together by mutual blessings. Israel is blessed as the chosen nation, chosen to be a kingdom of priests on behalf of the nations. The nations receive the blessing of Israel's intercession and were to bless the one that was blessed Israel), and so receive a blessing back.

Psalm 67 illustrates how this relationship is intended to function:

> *"God be merciful to us and bless us, And cause His face to shine upon us, Selah That Your way may be known on earth, Your salvation among all nations. Let the peoples praise You, O God; Let all the peoples praise You. Oh, let the nations be glad and sing for joy! For You shall judge the people righteously, and govern the nations on earth. Selah let the peoples praise You, O God; Let all the peoples*

praise You. Then the earth shall yield her increase; God, our own God, shall bless us. God shall bless us, and all the ends of the earth shall fear Him." (Ps. 67:1–7 NKJV)

Psalm 67 is the interplay between Israel and the nations. Israel entreats HaShem for the blessing of His presence. This request in Psalm 67:1 hearkens back to the priestly blessing of Numbers 6:22-27:

"The LORD spoke to Moses, saying, 'Speak to Aaron and his sons, saying, Thus you shall bless the people of Israel: you shall say to them, The LORD bless you and keep you; the LORD make his face to shine upon you and be gracious to you; the LORD lift up his countenance upon you and give you peace.' So shall they put my name upon the people of Israel, and I will bless them." (Num. 6:22–27)

The priests were commanded by HaShem to bless the people of Israel. The priests were commanded to invoke this blessing over the nation so that HaShem would place His name on the people. This is a blessing reserved for Israel. It is a demonstration of HaShem's covenant fidelity to be Israel's God and for Israel to be His people.

Psalm 67:1 is Israel's prayer for the release of this blessing upon the nation. But notice the outcome: *"So that your way may be known on earth and your salvation among all nations"* (Ps. 67:2). Israel seeks the blessing of HaShem's presence so that His salvation would be known among all nations. The dynamic is clear; when Israel is blessed the nations are blessed. But the blessing reciprocates back again from the nations to

Israel: *"Let the peoples[17] praise you, O God; let all the peoples praise you. Then the earth shall yield her increase; God, our own God will bless us"* (Ps. 67:5,6).

According to Jewish tradition, Psalm 67 is recited throughout the 49 days of counting the omer between Pesach and Shavuot.[18] This is the seven-week period between the barley harvest, which begins approximately at Pesach, and the wheat harvest, which begins approximately at Shavuot. The counting of the omer, among other things is a daily intercession for the wheat harvest to come. Israel's intercession for the wheat harvest, for *"the earth to yield her increase"* (Ps. 67:6), ties this bounty of the land to HaShem's blessings on the nations.

When the "peoples" praise the God of Israel, the land of Israel yields a bountiful harvest for the people of Israel. How fitting that the feast associated with the transmission of the Torah at Mt Sinai and the outpouring of the Holy Spirit in Jerusalem reflects the reciprocal blessing between Israel and the nations. Israel's blessing is the conduit for HaShem's *"way [to] be known on earth"* and His salvation *"among all nations"* (Ps. 67:2).

To recap: Israel is blessed with the result that the nations are blessed (verses 1,2). Then the nations are blessed with the result that Israel is blessed (verses 3-6). The psalm ends with Israel's blessedness resulting in the blessings flowing back to the nations yet again, "all the earth shall fear Him" (verse 7).

---

[17] In the Hebrew Scriptures the word "peoples" (Heb. עמים *ammim*), is usually used synonymously with "nations"

[18] "More on the Counting of the Omer" http://www.chabad.org/library/article_cdo/aid/1677/jewish/More-on-the-Omer.htm

Include in letter to CVC

The pattern of mutual blessing is to go on and on with blessing flowing back and forth and back and forth in greater and greater measure. That is the beautiful plan of HaShem.

This plan is an expression of HaShem's own nature. Within the Godhead reciprocal blessings continue to flow back and forth. The Father loves the Son and blesses him. The Son obeys the Father. The Father is blessed by the Son's obedience and blesses the Son. The Son is blessed by the Father's love and obeys the Father...on and on it goes, blessing after blessing, from glory to glory without end. The blessings flow back and forth and back and forth in greater and greater measure.

This is also the same pattern of mutual blessing reflected in the relationship between husband and wife and parents and children. Blessing the other results in a reciprocal blessing flowing back to the one who gave the blessing. There is much more one could say on this matter of mutual blessing but for our purposes we are focusing on this pattern as it pertains to Israel and the nations.[19] Israel is chosen and blessed but always with the nations in view. When Israel is blessed, it is for the sake of the nations, that they may be blessed.

Consider Moses' intercession after the golden calf incident. HaShem is ready to destroy the whole nation and begin again with Moses. Moses does not lead out with, "HaShem; please relent from destroying this people, remember your covenant with Abraham, Isaac and Jacob. These are your people..." No, Moses begins by reminding HaShem that if He were to destroy Israel then the Egyptians would get the wrong

---

[19] For further study: Daniel Juster. "Mutual Blessings" (Clarksville, MD: Lederer Books, 2013)

impression of HaShem's saving acts. Moses is asking HaS to spare Israel for the sake of the Egyptians:

> *"But Moses implored the* Lord *his God and said, 'O* Lord, *why does your wrath burn hot against your people, whom you have brought out of the land of Egypt with great power and with a mighty hand? Why should the Egyptians say, 'With evil intent did he bring them out, to kill them in the mountains and to consume them from the face of the earth?'"* (Exod. 32:10–12)

If Israel is to be the priestly nation on behalf of all the nations then if Israel is destroyed, HaShem's plan for the nations is thwarted. The relationship between Israel and the nations is so inextricably tied into the plan of God that one cannot exist without the other. In Acts 17, Paul explains to the Athenians that from one man HaShem made every nation. That is, the nations are HaShem's idea:

> *"And He has made from one blood every nation of men to dwell on all the face of the earth, and has determined their pre-appointed times and the boundaries of their dwellings, so that they should seek the Lord, in the hope that they might grope for Him and find Him."* (Acts 17:26–27)

HaShem determined their allotted times. That is, their seasons of influence (see, Jer. 1:9,10; Dan. 4:17), and their geographical boundaries. Paul explained that HaShem did this *"that they should seek the Lord, in the hope that they might grope for*

Him and find Him" (Acts 17:27). God created the nations so that they may be saved. Paul's declaration to the Athenians on God's authorship of all nations is based on the Song of Moses found at the end of Deuteronomy:

> *"When the Most High divided their inheritance to the nations, When He separated the sons of Adam, He set the boundaries of the peoples according to the number of the children of Israel."* (Deut. 32:8)[20]

The Song of Moses attributes the nations to HaShem's intentions, noting that HaShem gave each nation an inheritance. This corresponds to the "pre-appointed times" of Acts 17:26. That HaShem set the boundaries of the peoples corresponds to the *"boundaries of their dwellings"* (Acts 17:26). But whereas in Acts 17, Paul explains that this is so the nations might find the creator, in Deuteronomy this is according to the number of the "Children of Israel."

Paul paraphrased the Torah portion to explain that HaShem's purpose for the nations was to seek after and find God. The Song of Moses does not delve into HaShem's purpose for establishing the nations but explains that when HaShem purposed to establish the nations, He did so with Israel in mind. Later, we shall consider Paul's letter to the Ephesians. Here Paul explains that Israel and the nations together has been God's plan prior to creation. Salvation for

---

[20] NKJV. Some modern translations based on the critical text have "Sons of God" instead of "Children of Israel" but the MS Hebrew text is "לְמִסְפַּר בְּנֵי יִשְׂרָאֵל" (Deut. 32:8). According to the number of B'nai Yisrael (Sons of Israel).

both Israel and the nations is tied to their relationship together as One New Man in Messiah.

We see the same dynamic at work in the promise of Israel's restoration. In Ezekiel 36, HaShem made it clear that He will restore Israel despite their disobedience, but He was also careful to explain that this gracious response is not for Israel's sake:

> *"Therefore say to the house of Israel, Thus says the Lord GOD: 'I do not do this for your sake, O house of Israel, but for My holy name's sake, which you have profaned among the nations wherever you went. And I will sanctify My great name, which has been profaned among the nations, which you have profaned in their midst; and the nations shall know that I am the LORD,' says the Lord GOD, when I am hallowed in you before their eyes.* [21] *"*
> (Ezek. 36:22–23)

What is perhaps most astounding about this passage is that HaShem not only promised to act on Israel's behalf to bring them back to the land but that this bringing back hallows HaShem's name for the sake of the Gentiles. HaShem has the holiness of His name in view but the good He does for Israel, bringing them back to the land and once there, filling them with His Holy Spirit, is so the nations will know that HaShem is God.

---

[21] Some modern translations translate "hallowed in you" as "hallowed through you". The Hebrew preposition can fit for both translations. However, the idea of hallowed "in" Israel fits better with the context (see, Ezek. 36:25,26).

All this grace towards Israel is not for Israel's sake, but for the sake of the nations. As a Messianic Jew I burn with passion for the church to recognize that HaShem is restoring Israel in our day. Often, my zeal is related to the church's ambivalence towards Israel and the Jewish people, and yet, this restoration that stirs my spirit is not so much for me and my people, but for the nations, that they would know that the God of Israel is the maker of heaven and earth.

All of HaShem's dealings with Israel, from choosing Abraham and the Patriarchs, to their deliverance from Egypt, to sparing them in the wilderness, to restoring them back to the land, all these gracious acts to Israel have been conceived with the nations in view. Israel is for the sake of the nations and as we shall discover later when we explore the Book of Romans, in a similar respect, the nations are for the sake of Israel. This reciprocal relationship of mutual blessing is One New Man, and it has been God's plan from the beginning.

Yeshua's last great command to his disciples was to take the gospel to the ends of the earth and make disciples of all nations. The Jewish envoys of the New Covenant, the covenant promised to Israel were to look beyond the needs of their own people to take the message of salvation to the nations.

In church parlance we call this the Great Commission and understand it to be the prime mandate of the Church. I am not disputing this but it reflects only one side of the divine mandate to bring all things together in Messiah. The Gentiles must be gathered but the Jews must be gathered too. Isaiah 11 spells out Messiah's dual mandate.

Isaiah 11 begins with the promise that from the 'stum Jesse, Messiah will come. This 'anointed one' will establi... kingdom where *the earth shall be full of the knowledge of the* LORD *as the waters cover the sea*" (Isa. 11:9).

The passage continues with two verses that begin with *"In that day."* In that day the Messiah will stand as a banner for the peoples, that is the Gentiles (Isa. 11:10), and in that day the Messiah will *"assemble the outcasts of Israel, and gather the dispersed of Judah from the four corners of the earth"* (Isa. 11:12). Messiah is both the banner that the Gentiles will seek and the gatherer of dispersed Israel back from the four corners of the earth. This dual mandate is also demonstrated in Isaiah 49:

"And now the LORD *says, he who formed me from the womb to be his servant, to bring Jacob back to him; and that Israel might be gathered to him—for I am honoured in the eyes of the* LORD, *and my God has become my strength—he says: "It is too light a thing that you should be my servant to raise up the tribes of Jacob and to bring back the preserved of Israel; I will make you as a light for the nations, that my salvation may reach to the end of the earth."* (Isa. 49:5–6)

It is worth noting that this section of Isaiah begins by calling the nations to hear this prophecy: *"Listen to me, O coastlands, and give attention, you peoples from afar"* (Isa. 49:1). This oracle concerning the Messiah is a message directed to the Gentiles, those as Paul would later say are "afar off."

According to Isaiah 49:5,6, Yeshua was formed in the womb, that is, he was born, for a dual purpose. Yeshua's first mandate is to gather Jacob again, to bring Israel back (just as we read in Isa. 11:11,12). HaShem says that is not enough; there is another purpose too. That is, to gather the Gentiles as well, or as the scripture declares, the servant is to be God's light to the nations so that HaShem's salvation will reach to the ends of the earth (Just as we read in Isa. 11:10). No one is excluded, but neither are Jews and Gentiles lumped together with no distinction. The dual mandate is: Israel gathered back, and we should understand this both in a geographical and spiritual sense, and God's salvation to the ends of the earth.

We understand that the mandate to see God's salvation reach the ends of the earth translates into our direct responsibility to carry the message there. The Great Commission doesn't just happen – Messiah's mandate to be God's salvation for the nations is our mandate. The same is true for Messiah's mandate to bring about Israel's restoration.

This mandate is our mandate too. In the same way we are responsible to carry out Yeshua's mandate to the nations, we are also responsible to carry out Yeshua's mandate to facilitate Israel's restoration. This may seem like a radical proposition but again Isaiah helps clarify the role of the nations gathered to Israel's Messiah in accomplishing scattered Israel's restoration. In exile, Israel laments: *"But Zion said, 'The LORD has forsaken me; my Lord has forgotten me'"* (Isa. 49:14). HaShem's answer removes all doubt as to His unwavering commitment to His people.

"Can a woman forget her nursing child, that she should have no compassion on the son of her womb? Even these may forget, yet I will not forget you. Behold, I have engraved you on the palms of my hands; your walls are continually before me." (Isa. 49:15–16)

The idea that a nursing mother could forget her child would have been preposterous in Isaiah's day. A mother's love for her baby is the supreme example of commitment and fidelity and yet, even if such a thing could occur, HaShem's commitment is even more resolute. Even if such an abhorrent thing could occur that a mother would forsake her infant child, He could never forsake Israel. As He promised, He will gather them back — this is why Messiah was born. But just as Messiah born to be God's salvation to the ends of the earth requires His Body to *"Go into all the world and preach the gospel to every creature"* (Mark 16:15); so also, Israel regathered is a task His Body must embrace in Yeshua's name:

"Thus says the Lord GOD: 'Behold, I will lift up my hand to the nations, and raise my signal to the peoples; and they shall bring your sons in their arms, and your daughters shall be carried on their shoulders.'" (Isa. 49:22)

We are called to participate in both of Messiah's mandates. We take the Gospel to the ends of the earth and we carry Israel's exiled sons and daughters back in our arms and on our shoulders - Just as Israel and the nations are inextricably linked, so too Messiah's dual mandates are inextricably linked. This is the plan from the beginning. Abraham was chosen so

69

all the families of the earth would be blessed. Israel was chosen to be God's priestly nation on behalf of all nations. When Israel is blessed, the nations are blessed, when the nations are blessed, Israel is blessed. As God's people, both Jew and Gentile, we are called to participate in Messiah's dual mandate for Israel's restoration and the nations' salvation, for the sake of HaShem's great purpose, that *"the earth shall be full of the knowledge of the LORD as the waters cover the sea"* (Isa. 11:9).

Response: A small town pastor makes a life changing discovery

Rick Barker, Lead Pastor, Cariboo Christian Life Fellowship

Rick Barker is a former journalist turned pastor. He has been leading Cariboo Christian Life Fellowship (CCLF), an inter-denominational church in rural British Columbia, Canada for 25 years. I have known Rick for over 30 years. I served as an elder along with Rick prior to my wife Sue and I making Aliyah in 2005. (MS)

I was standing on stage in Jerusalem with about a dozen pastors whom I didn't know. It was the end of a weeklong prayer tour/conference in Israel – the very first time I had ever ventured to this land of the Bible, the heart of history. Prior to what God did in and through Marty and Sue, Israel was pretty much out of my grid in my day-to-day thinking. I had some sense of the importance of Israel, especially in the last days, and I knew that God loved the land of Israel but I was busy pastoring a few hundred people, had our ministries going on every week, and was pretty much focused on my own little strip of land in the Kingdom of God.

The Shoubs were our longtime friends and we were supporting them in Israel but that was about it. I was talking to Marty on the phone one afternoon and asked him, "so what's next for us as, you know, a supportive Gentile church in Canada?" His response was extremely quick. "You need to come," he said. "Come and see."

That was not what I was expecting, but it seemed to lodge into my heart and stuck there. And through several providential, seeming coincidences, my wife Marci and I and a good friend who helped make it happen, made the long journey to a conference-tour hosted in part by Marty himself at the Tents of Mercy Congregation where he was on staff.

Now following a week of touring, praying and learning, it was the final day of the conference. We had seen a myriad of ancient sites, each site carrying a bigger 'wow-factor' than the one we experienced the day before; we heard much teaching, watched ancient prophecies being fulfilled right before our eyes, heard the heart cry of several Israeli pastors, mini-testimonies of IDF soldiers and even young people who were just about to embark on their three-year tour of duty in the IDF – this was all very impacting, in fact, more than I knew.

For the first time, as I stood there on that stage, it began to hit me all at once — It felt like a tsunami of thoughts and ideas pounding against the shores of my soul. I began to comprehend just how active God was working in modern-day Israel. Israelis born and raised in Israel were now coming to faith in Yeshua in great numbers. I felt like

I was witnessing the Biblical Book of Acts coming alive in a whole new way, reading the Bible "in colour" so to speak instead of black and white.

To say I was overwhelmed at that moment is an understatement. And, now, here I was on the stage at the end of this conference and along with my fellow pastor delegates I was asked a question I really didn't have an answer for: *"how has this tour affected you as a pastor?"*

I was about ninth down the line of about a dozen pastors, and the microphone was getting closer and closer to me all the time. As it got closer, I could feel my chest start lifting and tears welling up in the corners of my eyes. As I tried to suppress these emotions, my anxiety only continued to deepen – I knew something serious was going on inside my soul, pulsating deep within me. But all I could think was, "What is going on?" I was overwhelmed with the sense or revelation that "this right here"... not the "this" of a conference but THIS-WHOLE-BIG-PICTURE - The "THIS" of what God was doing in Israel right now in my time, WAS THE MOST IMPORTANT THING GOING ON IN THE EARTH TODAY!

I know that statement may have seemed a little dramatic but I could not get it out of my head – it just kept boiling up in my innermost parts. Fervency. This was no ordinary moment for me; it was a Kingdom moment and God was pressing it upon my soul. The more I thought about these things the more I realized that importance of Jew and Gentile together. As I reflect on that time waiting for my turn at the microphone I consider what Marty said in this chapter:

"As a Messianic Jew I burn with passion for the church to recognize that HaShem is restoring Israel in our day. Often, my zeal is related to the church's ambivalence towards Israel and the Jewish people, and yet, this restoration that stirs my spirit is not so much for me and my people, but for the nations, that they would know that the God of Israel is the maker of heaven and earth."

God was truly bringing back the Jewish people from the nations like He said He would and the mystery of the One New Man is literally unfolding in our day and rushing us toward the return of Messiah a whole lot sooner than I had previously thought. These were the sorts of thoughts that were racing through my mind as the microphone was approaching. Tears started flowing like someone turned on the sprinkler and I said, "I have missionaries we support all around the world, and efforts we are making every week locally... but this, *THIS,* I don't know what I'm supposed to do with this at all."

Following the meeting a nice old Jewish man, classic long salt-n-pepper curly beard, a twinkle in his eye and a friendly smile, walked up to me, gave me a hug and said in a Russian-Israeli accent, "don't vhorry my friend, Godt vhill show you vhaat to do." And he nodded very knowingly, smiled, and walked away.

That was some time ago. Since that first memorable trip I have been to Israel 10 times, participating in several Tikkun International conferences and organized my own tours to help pastor friends and congregants catch a sense of what God is doing in Israel and with the Jewish people.

God is still showing me "vhaat to do" in terms of this beautiful country Israel and His incredible people. I still feel a call to do my part in 'awakening the west' to what God is in Israel with His Living Stones, and to be a part of the of linking Jew and Gentile as the One New Man that Paul writes about in Ephesians 2.

Marty wrote: *"if Israel is destroyed, God's plan for the nations is thwarted. The relationship between Israel and the nations is so inextricably tied into the plan of God that one cannot exist without the other."*

How important is that in our day and time? When every surrounding nation is pointing their guns at Israel, when governments from all over the globe are pressing on Israel, this impacts me as a Gentile. The destiny of the planet is wrapped up in this little country on the eastern shore of the Mediterranean. We need Israel and the Jewish people, and they need us. This reality causes me to amplify my prayer life for Messianic congregations in Israel, as well as Israeli government authorities.

I believe the One New Man is a deep concern on the heart of the Lord in these days… but as Marty explained, this is not a new concern. It has been on the heart of the Lord from the very start − all of what He has done in and through Israel to bring forth Messiah, and what He is currently doing in and through Israel now is for the blessing of us all.

I think many believers have some understanding of this concept, but in my opinion, the Body of Christ needs a much greater understanding of this current move of God in restoring the Jewish people back to their land and once in the land, opening up their hearts to Yeshua. Many simply believe that all was fulfilled in Him, without thinking through how Jesus' death and resurrection relates to Israel's spiritual and physical restoration.

As I understand Romans 11, Israel's restoration will mean life from the dead, not only for the Jewish people but for the rest of the world as well – we will see an authentic revival move of God as Jew and Gentile together clue in to the mystery of the One New Man. It is my prayer that the revelation of the mystery of One New Man will soon come to fulfillment in the Jewish people and the Body of Christ in the nations.

CHAPTER 3

Paul's Explanation of the Mystery

The Hebrew scriptures anticipate a glorious consummation of God's purposes for humanity and even the natural world, as Isaiah anticipates, "the earth will be filled with the knowledge of the Lord," analogous to the waters covering the seas (Isa. 11:19). In his letter to the Ephesians, Paul relates this grand consummation to a mystery. The mystery of the Gospel is cast in terms of Jewish/Gentile relationships but its ultimate goal goes much further than removing the wall of partition separating these two groups. The purpose of the Mystery is ultimately to bring about the consummate restoration of all things in Messiah. The "mystery" now revealed is our Heavenly Father's ultimate purpose:

> *"He lavished upon us, in all wisdom and insight making known to us the mystery of his will, according to his purpose, which he set forth in Christ as a plan for the fullness of time, to unite all things in him, things in heaven and things on earth."*
> (Eph. 1:8–10)

The mystery of His will is that He has purposed to unite all things, in both heaven and earth in Messiah Yeshua. That is a very heady purpose indeed, a purpose beyond Jews and Gentiles to include "all things," but at the same time a purpose that is worked out through uniting Jews and Gentiles in Messiah as One New Man.

It is beyond my understanding to speak with confidence about the details on gathering angels and powers in the heavenly realms together in Messiah but with respect to gathering the *"things on earth,"* those to be gathered are divided into Jews and Gentiles. This may seem like an arbitrary division or even an inaccurate reckoning. There are other ways one might describe divisions within humanity: male and female, rich and poor, race, language, religion, culture…There are many facets to the human condition but whatever differences we might have, when you peel back the layers, our differences pale in comparison to our shared sameness. Yet, the division of humanity as reckoned in scripture makes the distinction between Israel and the nations.

The English word "Gentiles" is a translation of the Hebrew word for nations (*Goyim*). "Gentiles" in its original sense in the Hebrew Bible does not convey any negative judgment. Rather, it is the term Israel uses to distinguish itself from all other nations. Because there has been some confusing teaching these days making a distinction between Jews and Israel[22] I should note that since Persian times the designation

---

[22] It is beyond the scope of this book to make a thorough critique of "Two House" theology. However, for those who may have some concerns as to whether there is an end time company known as Israel and another known as Judah, I would recommend the following critique presented to the

"Jews" is equivalent to Israel. When Paul speaks about the Jews, he is not making a distinction between Jews and Israel (Please compare Rom. 9:24 and 9:27); the terms are synonymous in both post-exilic Old Testament and New Testament parlance.

The scriptures divide humanity between Israel and the nations. Balaam, under the inspiration of the Holy Spirit declares, *"For from the top of the crags I see him, from the hills I behold him; behold, a people dwelling alone, and not counting itself among the nations"* (Num. 23:9). Moses reminds the Lord, *"For how shall it be known that I have found favour in your sight, I and your people? Is it not in your going with us, so that we are distinct, I and your people, from every other people on the face of the earth?"* (Exod. 33:16). The Psalmist wrote, *"He declares his word to Jacob, his statutes and rules to Israel. He has not dealt thus with any other nation"* (Ps. 147:19–20). Jeremiah proclaims, *"For thus says the LORD: 'Sing aloud with gladness for Jacob, and raise shouts for the chief of the nations'"* (Jer. 31:7).

Israel stands alone, not reckoned among the nations (or as Jeremiah so designated), as the special nation among all nations. But as we covered last chapter, the distinction is not absolute because God chose Israel with the nations in view.

There are many other examples of this division throughout the scriptures and we covered a number of these in our last chapter. A careful reading of the scriptures reveals this interplay between Israel and the nations throughout the entire canon of scripture from Genesis to Revelation. The last book in the canon, Revelation, describes the great throng from the

International Messianic Jewish Alliance:
http://www.seedofabraham.org/downloads/ephraimite%20error.pdf

nations (Rev. 7:9), and a much smaller company from Israel's tribes (Rev. 7:4). This distinction serves to highlight Israel's unique status among the nations but there is more here than simply affirming Israel's election. Israel's election is always related to blessings for the nations. Abraham is blessed, but this is so that in him, *"all the families of the earth shall be blessed"* (Gen. 12:3). This blessing ultimately comes through faith in Yeshua the Messiah.

Paul reminds the Gentiles in Ephesians chapter 2 that prior to salvation in Yeshua, the condition of the Gentiles was anything but blessed:

> *"Therefore remember that at one time you Gentiles in the flesh, called 'the uncircumcision' by what is called the circumcision, which is made in the flesh by hands— remember that you were at that time separated from Christ, alienated from the commonwealth of Israel and strangers to the covenants of promise, having no hope and without God in the world."* (Eph. 2:11–12)

The language Paul uses here could not be more telling, "separated...alienated...strangers...no hope, without God in the world." Paul goes on to speak of a partition being removed; this is a reference to the wall in the Temple complex that had barred entrance to Gentiles from entering the court of Israel. Gentiles were permitted to worship at the Temple but they could only go so far. A barrier warned any Gentile that should he pass into this "Israel only" area he would be responsible for his own death.

The removal of the barrier is solely for the benefit of Gentiles; it does not affect Israel's status as the people of God. The barrier kept Gentiles out. Israel already enjoyed the status as the recipients of the covenants of promise and people of God. Despite Israel's many failures, hope endured because of God's faithfulness. He had promised to never forsake Israel (Deut. 31:6) and never abandon His covenant fidelity towards them (Lev. 26:44). But in Messiah the people of God expands beyond natural Israel to include the nations that heretofore had been excluded from God's covenant family. Those who were far off have been brought near (Eph. 2:13).

Paul would certainly understand the ramifications of this barrier. He wrote this letter while imprisoned for allegedly taking Trophimus, a Gentile behind the very barrier he is referring to here. In Messiah, this barrier has been abolished; the Gentiles are now "joined...connected...family...full of hope...adopted by our Heavenly Father." There is no small irony here that the charge which landed Paul in prison was on account of the accusation falsely leveled against him of taking a Gentile beyond this barrier (See, Acts 21:21-36 for Luke's account of this event). While awaiting trial before Caesar on this trumped up charge, Paul wrote the Letter to the Ephesians. Perhaps this event was on his mind when he wrote the Ephesians to encourage them in their new status in Messiah.

Paul describes this as the creation in Messiah of "One New Man" (Eph. 2:15). The image lends itself to the idea of metamorphosis. Whereas, once, prior to the cross there were Jews and Gentiles, now there is a new identification, "One New Man". Certainly, this is the message of Ephesians 2:15

but we need to be very careful about how we understand what are the characteristics of this One New Man. This Pauline term does not mean that Jewish and Gentile identity no longer exists. Perhaps you are thinking, "This is exactly what Paul wrote in Galatians 3:28 - *'There is neither Jew nor Greek, there is neither slave nor free, there is no male and female, for you are all one in Christ Jesus.'"*

Let's consider Paul's sometimes frustratingly difficult way of holding two seemingly opposite truths together in tension. Peter gave us some good advice when he reminded us that in Paul's writings, *"There are some things in them that are hard to understand"* (2 Pet. 3:16). Paul has the sometimes exasperating communication style of affirming the truth of seeming opposites, he is the champion of grace (Eph. 2:8), and yet he declares men shall be judged according to their works (Rom. 2:6); He affirms the sovereignty of God (Rom. 9:16), and also affirms the free will of mankind (Rom. 12:1ff). Sometimes, truth has a complex dimension to it. Can it be that God is sovereign, and has predestined us to be conformed to the image of His son and at the same time we are to work out our salvation with fear and trembling? That we are saved by grace and yet we will be judged by our works?

If we consider the whole counsel of God these seeming contradictions are not a problem for us — just as Yeshua is fully God and fully man and it is both wrong and right to answer a fool in his folly (see Prov. 26:4,5). Divine truth is complicated, and sometimes does not boil down to simple propositions. Sometimes, and this is especially the modus operandi of Jewish learning, the truth needs to be teased out by considering both sides of a complex issue such as grace and works. We are fond of trying to boil everything down to simple answers. Sometimes the truth does boil down to a simple answer, but sometimes it does not – see what I mean about two sides of truth sometimes needing to be held in tension? If we understand this dynamic of truths in tension we will go a long way towards understanding the "hard to understand" writings of the Apostle Paul.

It is true that in Messiah, Jew and Gentile no longer exist, but in the same way that in Messiah, male and female no longer exist and servant and master no longer exist. One New Man does not dissolve Jew and Gentile identity anymore than being in Messiah dissolves male and female identity. Our Father's unity does not mean uniformity. A man and a woman joined together in marriage become one flesh, and yet at the same time they maintain a uniqueness that we are to honour and cherish. So too with One New Man. Jew and Gentile are joined together in Messiah Yeshua and at the same time carry unique callings, gifting and identity.

As mentioned above, the imagery of Ephesians 2 does not describe a change in position for Israel - the abolishment of the wall of partition brings Gentiles, those who at one time were excluded, within the circle of the covenants of promise. Those who had no hope, and were "without God" have been brought near by the blood of Yeshua. Israel already enjoyed this position but achieves a new status by having those in the nations join them in Messiah as the people of God.

I should clarify that though Israel enjoys status as the people of God, Israel's salvation in only assured by the blood of Yeshua. As Peter explained to the Jewish leaders, *"there is salvation in no one else, for there is no other name under heaven*

83

given among men by which we must be saved" (Acts 4:12). The issue of Israel's status as God's people and individual salvation is a large, important topic beyond the scope of this book. Israel as a nation enjoys covenant status as God's people but salvation for individual Jews is (as with Gentiles) only through application of Yeshua's atonement. The promise of scripture is that *"all Israel will be saved"* (Rom. 11:26; Isa. 45:17). This is also according to the Father's purpose to make One New Man in Yeshua.[23]

The blood of Yeshua does not abolish Jewish or Gentile identity but it does abolish the enmity between Jew and Gentile (Eph. 2:16). There is no room for Gentile envy anymore because now the Gentiles share in Israel's covenants of promise. There is no room for Jewish pride anymore because we cannot make an exclusive claim to the covenants of promise beyond what Yeshua's death and resurrection has accomplished for the Gentiles. So much of the enmity between Jews and Gentiles has arisen out of envy and pride. Both Jews and Gentiles have fallen into these debilitating attitudes because we have all failed to recognize that our uniqueness is not for the sake of exclusivity but rather for mutually reciprocating blessings. Gentiles have no reason to envy Jewish choseness

because in the first place, this choosing was for the sake of the Gentiles and in the second place, has now expanded in Messiah to include those from the nations.

Likewise choseness was never grounds for Jewish exclusivity. Judaism does not promote Jewish exclusivity — the Sages understood Israel's choseness was for all humanity and

---

[23] For further reference see David H. Stern. "The Church's biggest Challenge" *Israel's Restoration* Vol. 18, No 8 (August 2009): 4,6

Jewish prayers anticipate all the nations eventually coming under God's banner. The last prayer in the synagogue prayer service is the *Alenu* (it is our duty). The prayer concludes with an intercession for the nations declaring, "They (the Nations), will accept the yoke of Your kingdom, and You will reign over them soon and for ever...And it is said: 'Then the Lord shall be King over all the earth; and on that day the Lord shall be One and His name One.'"[24] Despite what our Sages teach, we Jews must guard against a misplaced pride that assumes we were chosen because we possessed some merit (see Deut. 7:7). As Yeshua reminded us, *"And do not presume to say to yourselves, 'We have Abraham as our father,' for I tell you, God is able from these stones to raise up children for Abraham"* (Matt. 3:9).

God's sovereign choosing of the one is always for the sake of the many. As we will see below, in chapter 5 on Paul's letter to the Romans, Jews and Gentiles complete each other and enable each other to fulfill their destinies. Jews need Gentiles to fulfill their destiny and likewise Gentiles need Jews for the same reason. Regrettably, history demonstrates that the enmity Yeshua's cross abolished between Jew and Gentile has continued on between Jews and Gentiles. This is not to say that Yeshua's cross did not abolish this enmity, rather, due to our own pride and unbelief, both Jews and Gentiles have failed to appropriate this grace accomplished through Messiah's atoning death.

There remains an enmity between Jews and Gentiles; to our shame, even in the Body of Messiah. There is no place for Anti-Semitism or Jewish nationalist pride within the Body of

---

[24] "The Koren Siddur" First Bilingual Edition. Translation by Rabbi Jonathan Sachs. (Jerusalem: Koren Publishers Jerusalem ltd. 2009) 182

Messiah. The blood of Yeshua has removed the enmity, woe to us if we build up again what HaShem has torn down. I will address this matter further in the next chapter.

The blood of Messiah establishes shalom for both Jews and Gentiles in Messiah. A hostility that grew out of mutual distrust, from misplaced envy and pride is abolished in Messiah. The conditions for the gathering of all things on earth are now possible. The nations now have access to the covenants, which include them in the people of God. [25] Likewise, Jewish covenant status does not automatically ensure spiritual regeneration; this is achieved for both Jews and Gentiles in Messiah Yeshua - *"For through him we both have access in one Spirit to the Father"* (Eph. 2:18–19).

This is the mystery Paul received by revelation alone in the Arabian Desert. A message for the Gentiles that in Messiah they are fellow heirs with Israel, members of the same body and now partakers of the promise that had at one time been Israel's exclusive domain (Eph. 3:1-7). This is the mysterious plan of God which he put into effect, even before the world began, the plan that ultimately leads to the unity of "all things, in both heaven and earth in Messiah Yeshua" (See, Eph. 1:9,10).

This One New Man in Messiah demonstrates HaShem's wisdom to the heavenly realm (Eph. 3:10). We often think of this scripture in light of what Paul told the Corinthians:

---

[25] It is worth mentioning that even the New Covenant belongs to Israel (Jer. 31:31). The terms of the covenant provide for its expansion to include all peoples.

Yet among the mature we do impart wisdom, although it is not a wisdom of this age or of the rulers of this age, who are doomed to pass away. But we impart a secret and hidden wisdom of God, which God decreed before the ages for our glory. None of the rulers of this age understood this, for if they had, they would not have crucified the Lord of glory. (1 Cor. 2:6–8)

Indeed, the mystery of the One New Man is a witness against the rulers of this age, *"the spirit at work in the sons of disobedience"* (Eph. 2:2). God's wisdom to bring both Jews and Gentiles together in Messiah is a powerful indictment against the demonic realm of the victory assured over the serpent promised in the very beginning (Gen. 3:15). But this display of wisdom is not just for the demonic realm. The heavenly realm is in fact more the domain of good angels than it is of evil ones. What message is conveyed to HaShem's angelic host by the unfolding of this mystery? If we see this mystery in reference to *"the mystery of His will"* (Eph. 1:9), then the wisdom displayed is the gathering of those "on earth" towards HaShem's ultimate purpose of gathering earth and heaven together in Messiah Yeshua (Eph. 1:10).

The unity of Jew and Gentile in Messiah (God's servants on earth) reflects and exemplifies the unity of God's servants in heaven. When earth and heaven agree, the power, wisdom and love of God is activated towards fulfilling the will of God done on earth as it is in heaven. Angels are *"ministering spirits sent out to serve for the sake of those who are to inherit salvation"* (Heb. 1:14). When the church functions as One New Man, Jew and Gentile as heirs together, then the heavenly realm is activated to assist these Jewish and Gentile heirs of salvation to fulfill their destiny and conform to heaven's will.

We see an example of the angelic realm coming to aid Daniel when he conformed to Heaven's will. In Daniel 9 we learn that by reading the scroll of Jeremiah Daniel understood that Israel's exile was to last seventy years (see, Jer. 25:12). Daniel knew the exile was soon to be over but he also knew that the Torah stated that Israel would only return from exile if they first turned back to HaShem in repentance:

> *"And when all these things come upon you, the blessing and the curse, which I have set before you, and you call them to mind among all the nations where the LORD your God has driven you, and return to the LORD your God, you and your children, and obey his voice in all that I command you today, with all your heart and with all your soul, then the LORD your God will restore your fortunes and have mercy on you, and he will gather you again from all the peoples where the LORD your God has scattered you."*
> (Deut. 30:1–3)

Daniel's reaction to the specified 70 year duration of the exile was not to check the calendar to see how many more days, months, and years were left until the seventy years turned over on the heavenly chronometer. Instead, immediately after reading that the exile was to end after seventy years, Daniel obeyed the will of Heaven by pouring out his heart in repentance for the sake of his people. This was not just an intercessors' reaction to the possibility of the exile ending soon, it was a man of God knowing the divine will and obeying scripture's commands. Daniel's intercessory prayer is a beautiful example of identification repentance. I am sure Daniel's intercession was necessary for Jeremiah's prophecy to be fulfilled. But notice the immediate effect of Daniel's prayer.

> "*While I was speaking and praying, confessing my sin and the sin of my people Israel, and presenting my plea before the LORD my God for the holy hill of my God, while I was speaking in prayer, the man Gabriel, whom I had seen in the vision at the first, came to me in swift flight at the time of the evening sacrifice. He made me understand, speaking with me and saying, 'O Daniel, I have now come out to give you insight and understanding. At the beginning of your pleas for mercy a word went out, and I have come to tell it to you, for you are greatly loved. Therefore consider the word and understand the vision.'*"
> (Dan. 9:20–23)

As soon as Daniel displayed the wisdom of God to the heavenly realms by conforming to heaven's will, the angel Gabriel was dispatched to give him "wisdom and understanding." As the Body of Messiah we have sorely lacked this dimension of displaying the wisdom of God to the heavenly realms because we have not aligned ourselves properly to the will of heaven with respect to Jew and Gentile, fellow heirs together as One New Man.

There is much talk these days of heaven touching earth, of connection to the heavenly realm and also of the required unity in the church necessary for this powerful connection. Paul is saying this unity is all about God's mysterious plan to bring

Jew and Gentile together. In order for us to truly see the revival and activation of heaven's will done on earth, those called from among the Gentiles must see that God's plan and Messiah's body is not just the church in the nations but also those of God's ancient covenant people Israel. Likewise, those from among the stock of Abraham, Isaac and Jacob must recognize Israel has expanded to include all nations. This has always been HaShem's plan from the very beginning.

It breaks my heart that there is so little emphasis on the necessity of us realizing God's plan as One New Man to bring about the revival we all long for. How can we speak about Yeshua's John 17 prayer for our unity without emphasizing that such unity first manifests itself as Jew and Gentile together? How can we talk about heaven touching earth, about God's will done on earth as it is in heaven without acknowledging that the purpose HaShem established before the world began is for Jew and Gentile joined together in Messiah? We cannot achieve heaven's will on earth without coming in to order as One New Man. The release of angelic ministry is activated by our displaying the wisdom of God as Jew and Gentile, fellow heirs in Messiah. There are many wonderful believers who long to see heaven's will done on earth. May HaShem increase our understanding to recognize that the foundation for our oneness in Messiah and our conforming to the will of heaven is the church as One New Man in Messiah.

The church worldwide is beginning to wake up to this fundamental kingdom order but there is still staggering ignorance that has blinded our eyes to the truth. We will consider Paul's warning against arrogance and ignorance of the mystery of Israel later when we address Paul's letter to the Romans. It is important at this juncture for us to acknowledge that the connection between Israel and the nations is not a side issue for a few, perhaps overly zealous Christian Zionists but central to heaven's redemptive purposes.

Revivals have come and gone. They are a testimony to HaShem's grace and mercy and yet, inevitably they have not been sustained. The great outpouring at the end of the age is something else. It is HaShem's ultimate restoration purposes being fulfilled. We cannot consider these matters or expect to see their breakthrough without the church, and by that I mean both Jew and Gentile together in Messiah, coming into its divine patterned order. It is incumbent on us to re-align our motivation and understanding to follow the order heaven established from the beginning.

To do so is not so much about repentance and admitting failure (though these are components of required change), but more so, a new revelation of God's love and a renewed call to worship. After explaining the mystery of One New Man displaying God's wisdom to the heavenly realms, Paul pauses to worship the only wise God:

"This was according to the eternal purpose that he has realized in Christ Jesus our Lord, in whom we have boldness and access with confidence through our faith in him. So I ask you not to lose heart over what I am suffering for you, which is your glory.
For this reason I bow my knees before the Father, from whom every family in heaven and on earth is named." (Eph. 3:11–15)

It is because He *"was given, to preach to the Gentiles the unsearchable riches of Christ. To bring to light for everyone what is the plan of the mystery hidden for ages in God who created all things, so that through the church the manifold wisdom of God might now be made known to the rulers and authorities in the heavenly places"* (Eph. 3:8–10), that Paul bowed his *"knees before the Father."* Indeed, He bows before the Father *"from whom every family in heaven and earth is named"* (Eph. 3:14,15). Certainly, here Paul is alluding to the One New Man promise made to Abraham in Genesis 12:3.

It is because Paul was commissioned to reveal to the Gentiles that they were fellow heirs with Israel, and that this was HaShem's grand plan from the beginning that Paul must pause to worship. Moreover, the wonder of this plan compels Paul to pray for the Gentile church in Ephesus that, on account of this wonderful revelation they would be able to grasp *"what is the breadth and length and height and depth, and to know the love of Christ that surpasses knowledge, that you may be filled with all the fullness of God"* (Eph. 3:18–19). The plan has always been to gather a family from all nations. This is the love of our Heavenly Father. A love that initiated a plan that left no one out. A plan that meant the Son of God would taste death for everyone. As Yeshua Himself told us, *"For God so loved the world..."*

Response: The difference between a secret and a mystery

Sharon Hayton, Executive Director, CMJ Canada.

I have known Sharon for several years. She is a trusted colleague and was a co-leader along with Dean Bye and myself of the cross Canada initiative, Loving God, Blessing Israel. (MS)

There is nothing more exciting in terms of our walk with the Lord than to come to a new understanding of a truth from the Scriptures. These 'ah ha' moments come to us by revelation, the Holy Spirit opening our eyes to the truth, to understand what the Scripture is telling us — The mystery revealed.

In Biblical terms, a mystery is different from a secret. A mystery is something that God has alluded to in previous texts that is now made clear according to His Divine timing. As Marty Shoub has made clear in this chapter, the election of Israel as a Chosen Nation by God was always for the purpose of bringing light to the Nations. It was never just about the Jews, but through this nation God chose to be made known to all the nations.

In Ephesians Paul explains the mystery of the One New Man, which brings further understanding to God's purposes.

He would bring these two people groups together, which would bring an amazing revelation of His purposes even to the heavenly realms. His purpose of "gathering together in one all things in Christ, both which are in heaven and which are on earth – in Him" (Eph.1:10).

As the Gentiles cry out to God for revival, I agree with Marty who wrote, *"In order for us to truly see the revival and activation of heaven's will done on earth those called from among the Gentiles must see that God's plan and Messiah's body is not just the church in the nations but also those of God's ancient covenant people Israel."* For every revival there is a particular truth that God highlights for that time. Luther came to a new understanding of justification by faith before he led the reformation. For the Wesley awakening it was about holiness, that we can live a holy life in submission to God. And the Charismatic movement was based on the realization of the work of the Holy Spirit in and through believers. It was about God giving grace gifts, enabling the church to carry out its calling. So I believe, when there is a critical mass of believers that align themselves with God's heart for Jew and Gentile together in Christ, then revival will come.

Sadly, in my experience, there are many who are indifferent to the Jewish people. Some believe God is finished with the Jews, that the Church has replaced Israel in God's economy. They believe He is done with Israel. Anathema! This comes from bad teaching. It's so important that books like this are written and read to bring correction.

I shall never forget my first visit to Israel in the year 2000. As a pastor I had a slight interest in Israel as I did think the Jews to be part of God's plan, particularly since Jesus is Jewish.

But I had no concept of the unity brought about by the blood of Jesus. No concept of the relationship God desires us to have.

In fact, I had preached through the book of Ephesians and referenced it many times. It is one of my favourite books of the Bible. Yet, I did not grasp the revelation of the One New Man. I erroneously taught about unity from the texts, unity amongst denominations and between members of churches and so on. I believed this was very important, that the dividing walls were down and we were to demonstrate this through our relationships so the world would see our unity together as Christians. In so doing we would *"keep the unity of the Spirit and the bond of peace"* (Eph.4:3).

But I missed the big picture. I missed the context – to think God had brought Jew & Gentile together was there, but I did not really get the significance of it; that is, until I went to Israel.

As we traveled throughout the Land, as I witnessed what God was doing in our day, the restoration of the physical land, the return of His people, I found myself in a place of worship. God began to download into my heart the mystery. I didn't know the extent of it right away, but all I could do was bow down and worship.

We were asked by the leaders of our delegation to share about our experiences. I remember saying that I had no idea coming to Israel was about worship. But it was, and still is. God changed my heart. I began to have a love for the Jewish people that I couldn't explain. I've always loved the church because it is the Body of Christ. My understanding was expanding.

After being in Israel I realized that everything written, every detail of Scripture is true. And it will come to pass. God is faithful to fulfill His Word. When I returned to the Anglican congregation that I was pastoring I taught differently. I took them to the prophets and explained what I had witnessed in Israel. I intentionally shared the revelation of The One New Man. As a result, my congregation asked me if I would please take them to Israel. They wanted to receive my newfound revelation for themselves. I was thrilled. So the very next year off we went and had an amazing time together. God is faithful and blessed us in spades.

Now I had to deal with young people that wanted to move to Israel. Such a thing! One young man told me that he had fallen in love with the Israel of Jesus – it was all more than I could ask or imagine.

While we were in Jerusalem we stumbled on the mission of Christchurch in the Old City. Unknown to any of us, this is an Anglican mission that started in 1809 out of Britain. By the early 1800's they had gone to Israel to serve the Jewish people. They built the first hospital, the first school for girls, the first Protestant church in the Middle East. Their entire motivation came from the Scriptures. They realized that they could make a difference and through much prayer and sacrifice they certainly have. As Anglicans we were amazed, this was the best kept secret in Evangelical Christianity – the mission to the Jews starting so early, and by Anglicans no less. Truly these were the first Christian Zionists.

The Lord was connecting me with this mission. I knew it the minute I walked unto the property with my group. I kept this to myself, but I knew. A good relationship developed over the years, which resulted in them inviting me to Jerusalem to a visioning conference in 2007. They asked me then if I would bring Canada into the ministry of CMJ (Church's Ministry Amongst the Jews), a worldwide family all connected back to the multi-faceted mission of CMJ Israel, centred at Christchurch.

I had been wondering how I could ever bring all the passions the Lord had given me together - my passion for the Church, for our Nation of Canada and now for the Jewish people and the Nation of Israel.

God knew how, and He did it. As National Director of CMJ Canada I am fulfilling my destiny to serve the Lord in this particular calling. To reach out to the Jewish people, to teach within the Church regarding the place of Israel in God's redemptive plans, our responsibility as Gentile believers towards Israel and the Jewish people and to help the church see that "the manifold wisdom of God might be made known by the church to the principalities and powers in the heavenly realms" (Eph. 3:10).

This is the key to revival. My prayer is that more and more believers will chose to align themselves with God's heart as revealed in His Word so that His will be done on earth as it is in heaven.

I thank Marty Shoub for bringing the Mystery of "The One New Man" to light, for such a time as this.

CHAPTER 4

The Offence of Israel's Chosenness

"The difficulty we have with Israel's chosenness is not really about our theology. There is something that unsettles us to our core to think that God might chose one over another." I spoke those words at a very typical church in a very typical American city, full of good people doing their best to love God and love their neighbours. As I was speaking I caught the eye of a middle-aged woman in the fifth row. She was nodding her head in agreement and looking directly at me as if to say, "That is it, that is the problem for me".

All of us want to be chosen. There is something at the core of our being that rightly yearns for validation and acceptance. The truth that I am loved by God, and that He accepts me for who I am, regardless of my race, ethnicity, culture, gender or status speaks powerfully to our souls. There is something very right about our instinctual discomfort of some being preferred over others, especially when we consider God is love and that Yeshua gave his life because *"God so loved the world."*

The truth is that in Messiah, we are all chosen, all affirmed, all loved and accepted for whom we are as individuals. As I have stated previously, God's great purpose is to gather all of us together in Messiah (Eph. 1:5). Israel's chosenness has everything to do with this great divine purpose. Before we explore how the choosing of the one results in the choosing of all (we will address this when we look at the Book of Romans), I want to focus on the issue of offence at Israel's chosenness. I believe it is offence over Israel's exclusivity, however unconscious it may be, that lies at the heart of most people's difficulties with accepting and embracing Israel's chosenness – the issue is primarily about our discomfort with the idea of a unique chosen people and not an objection to the theological concept of God's sovereign election.

If there is a problem that goes beyond theology, which subtly pushes us away from embracing our call to show Israel mercy we should address it. But ultimately, if theology is not the problem it cannot be addressed by explanation and debate alone. Our discomfort over Israel's chosenness may be a healthy reaction to misunderstanding the purpose and responsibilities of chosenness. Once we understand what God's choosing really means, discomfort is replaced by gratitude for those bearing the yoke of chosenness. But it may also be something else, something sinister that hides just under the surface. It may be an offence stirred by envy and resentment. If this sort of offence is operating in our life the solution is to recognize it for what it is and repent. I think it is quite possible that many of us carry this sort of offence without being aware of it. Anti-Semitism has a spiritual root that affects Christians as much as anyone else. The sad record of church history bears that out.

This is a sensitive topic because it moves beyond the realm of explanation to addressing our emotions and maybe even our flaws. I am not standing in a place of judgment over anyone; believe it or not anti-Semitism can affect Jews too. I too have had to repent of my own anti-Semitism!

The offence of chosenness goes back to the very beginning. *"And the LORD had regard for Abel and his offering, but for Cain and his offering he had no regard"* (Gen. 4:4–5). In Genesis 4:4, the Hebrew reads literally, that HaShem looked upon Abel's sacrifice, his gaze was directed to the sacrifice He chose. Contrariwise, in Genesis 4:5, HaShem did not look at Cain's sacrifice; His gaze was averted from noting what Cain had presented. God chose Abel's sacrifice, Cain's offering was not chosen. Cain's envy of his brother Abel resulted in the first murder on the planet.

We see the same enmity between chosen Isaac and his brother Ishmael, and between chosen Jacob and his brother Esau. With these three sets of brothers, one was marked for favour and blessing and the other became envious and hateful. We see the same pattern with chosen Joseph and his brothers. Even within the "chosen" family those not chosen to a special place of prominence are tempted to envy and hate. The same envy lay behind Korah's rebellion against Moses (Num. 16:13).

The Jewish people have had to deal with this envy-induced hatred ever since they were chosen as HaShem's *"special treasure above all peoples"* (Exod. 19:5). The movie Fiddler on the Roof expresses a common Jewish reaction to being chosen. Tevya the milkman, as is his custom, carries on a one-way conversation with the Holy One as he walks down the road on his daily milk delivery runs. Reflecting on the difficulties he and his countrymen are facing because of Israel's chosenness, Tevya inquires of HaShem: "I know we are your chosen people but couldn't You choose someone else for a change?" Being chosen is not an exclusive shelter from difficulty. Being chosen by God is in fact a road of loneliness and suffering.

Paul the Apostle was chosen. We read in Acts that the apostles who came before him, though at first reticent to accept Paul, eventually embraced him as one of their own and rejoiced to hear of all God was doing through their new brother in the Lord. The Apostles give us a great example of a godly response to recognizing another's chosenness. Paul hadn't shared the hardships of those first disciples travelling on the road with Yeshua. He hadn't dropped everything and forsook all because he had found the Messiah. He wasn't one of the inner circle of three, he wasn't one of the twelve chosen *"to be with him"* (Mark 3:14), or one of the seventy sent out two by two to preach the gospel, he wasn't even one of the one hundred and twenty in the upper room. Just the opposite, he was a persecutor, an enemy of the apostles and the gospel. And yet, this one who was not a part of the inner circle of disciples was chosen to make a greater impact for the gospel than any of the apostles who came before him.

After Paul's revelation of Yeshua on the road to Damascus, Yeshua appeared to Ananias, a well regarded disciple in the city, and instructed him to seek Paul out and pray for him to receive his sight. Ananias protested, *"Lord, I have heard from many about this man, how much evil he has done to your saints at Jerusalem. And here he has authority from the chief priests to bind all who call on your name"* (Acts 9:13–14). Yeshua's response gives us a clear picture of the cost of chosenness: *"Go, for he is a chosen instrument of mine to carry my name before the Gentiles and kings and the children of Israel. For I will show him how much he must suffer for the sake of my name"* (Acts 9:15–16).

Paul was a chosen instrument, he would give his testimony before kings – even before Caesar, but his chosenness came with a steep price, he was chosen, *"to suffer many things"* for the sake of his Lord. Tradition tells us that all the apostles suffered martyrdom – they were all chosen, but none suffered the extremes that Paul did. The more auspicious the chosenness, the greater the suffering, we only have to look at Yeshua's example to know this is true.

The Jewish people are also an example of how chosenness and suffering go together. Suffering is a common reality for every people group and as individuals; all of us have suffered to some degree or another. The world is a beautiful place but human history is marked by suffering and cruelty – no one is exempt. However, the Jewish people are unique among all people groups, their history is burdened with suffering from their inception – even to the present day. Many people groups have suffered grave injustice and pain, but there is no other group that has such a consistent record of suffering, going back over such a long time period. Sometimes Jewish suffering has come as the consequences for disobedience. When HaShem chose Israel as a nation to be His special treasure, He set up an expectation of obedience that was rewarded with great blessing and conversely, He laid out a clear warning that disobedience would be punished.

However, it would be a serious mistake to conclude that all of Israel's sufferings are due to disobedience. Psalm 44 is a lament over Israel's great sufferings. The psalmist even compared Israel to sheep prepared for slaughter. The psalmist recounted a litany of suffering and deprivation, he then reminded HaShem, *"All this has come upon us, though we have not forgotten you, and we have not been false to your covenant. Our heart has not turned back, nor have our steps departed from your way"* (Ps. 44:17–18). Sometimes Israel has suffered not because they were disobedient but because they were obedient. Because they stood out from among the nations as a people set apart they have been a target for the scorn of others.

The ultimate covenant consequence of Israel's disobedience as set out in the Torah was exile from the land. The blessing and curse covenant promises of Leviticus 26 and Deuteronomy 28 both conclude with exile from the land:

> *"And I will scatter you among the nations, and I will unsheathe the sword after you, and your land shall be a desolation, and your cities shall be a waste."* (Lev. 26:33)

> *"And the LORD will scatter you among all peoples, from one end of the earth to the other, and there you shall serve other gods of wood and stone, which neither you nor your fathers have known."* (Deut. 28:64)

For a people to be scattered to the nations without a homeland usually meant the complete assimilation of that people within the larger people group — especially in the ancient world which lacked the sophisticated communications systems which now can offset the impact of assimilation.

However, the covenant HaShem made with Israel pro
that despite Israel's potential failure, HaShem Himself
never break convent with Israel. He would never utterly forsake
them:

> *"Yet for all that, when they are in the land of their*
> *enemies, I will not spurn them, neither will I abhor*
> *them so as to destroy them utterly and break my*
> *covenant with them, for I am the LORD their God.*
> *But I will for their sake remember the covenant with*
> *their forefathers, whom I brought out of the land of*
> *Egypt in the sight of the nations, that I might be their*
> *God: I am the LORD."* (Lev. 26:44–45)

The final outcome for disobedience should have meant
Israel's demise on account of assimilation. If Israel so
disobeyed as to completely reject their heritage and identity,
they would have simply faded into the mix of the Gentile
nations. If Israel went completely after the gods of the nations
then Israel would not have been distinguishable from the
nations, Israel would have ceased to exist.

But if Israel ceased to exist as a separate people, so too
their suffering on account of their being separate from the
nations would have ceased. Despite their failures, Israel never
completely gave up on being HaShem's people, and have
therefore faced the consequences of being set apart, even to
this day. We should understand Israel's preservation as the
result of HaShem's gracious protection — HaShem promised
to never allow Israel to fade into history (Lev. 26:44;
Jer. 31:35-37). Nevertheless, this gracious preservation of the

Jewish people has also meant that they have suffered for being HaShem's chosen people at the hands of envious Gentiles.

Israel's chosenness can create offence. It offends because it declares one over another. In a very real sense it strains against the truth that all people are made in God's image and therefore all belong to Him. To be very clear, I am not at all saying Israel's chosenness is truly offensive. God's choosing is not at all like human favouritism. It has nothing to do with a shallow incapacity to see value in all. God's choosing of the one is always, always for the sake of the many. If we can understand that Israel's chosenness is not a demonstration of God's capriciousness, but like Paul and Yeshua, a setting apart on behalf of others, then this offence is removed and replaced by deep gratitude. When we understand that Israel's chosenness was always on behalf of the nations, that God's special treasure above all people was to function as a kingdom of priests on behalf of the nations, then we understand that there is no offence against any other peoples' own value and dignity.

This is chosenness for the sake of others, and it is chosenness that has meant suffering on behalf of others, a suffering that brought forth great blessings to the nations. This is the message behind Romans 11. Israel, chosen of God becomes disobedient for the sake of the world. Israel's failure means salvation for the Gentiles, their rejection ushers in reconciliation for the world. They were broken off so that wild branches could be grafted in. We will address this in further detail when we consider the Book of Romans but it is enough to say now that the great blessings bestowed on the world by Israel's Messiah came at the expense of His own people.

The blessings Messiah intended for His people were not realized because Israel failed to recognize the day of their visitation.

> *"And when he drew near and saw the city, he wept over it, saying, 'Would that you, even you, had known on this day the things that make for peace! But now they are hidden from your eyes. For the days will come upon you, when your enemies will set up a barricade around you and surround you and hem you in on every side and tear you down to the ground, you and your children within you. And they will not leave one stone upon another in you, because you did not know the time of your visitation.'"* (Luke 19:41–44)

Imagine with me if you will. Yeshua is descending the Mount of Olives on the back of a Donkey's foal. The crowds are wildly cheering and proclaiming the Messianic invitation, *"Blessed is He who comes in the name of the LORD."* Yeshua and His entourage cross the Kidron Valley and enter Jerusalem through the Eastern Gate. There waiting for him stand Caiaphas and Annas and all the elders of Israel along with their wives and the children. They are all dressed in their finest clothes and they stand in rapt attention gazing at Yeshua as He dismounts from the foal. As He does so, they all prostrate themselves before Yeshua in solemn reverence. After a long silence Caiaphas humbly rises and with outstretched arms extends the welcome on behalf of the whole nation: "Master, we welcome you, blessed are you Messiah King who comes in the name of the Lord. Come now and ascend upon the throne of your father David and rule over us. We are your servants to command."

Forgive my over active imagination. Israel and especially Israel's leaders did not recognize the day of their visitation. If they could have, as Yeshua declared, He would have gathered them to Himself and they would have known a peace that still eludes them. Instead of peace they received terrifying consequences: The destruction of the Temple, the destruction of the city, exile, slavery and the long years of suffering in the diaspora.

Let us consider the consequences for the nations if Israel had been able to recognize the day of their visitation. Caiaphas welcomes Yeshua on behalf of the nation. Yeshua ascends up the golden stairs to the throne prepared for him. He would have been enthroned as Messiah, and his rule of righteousness, peace and justice would have begun. Israel's enemies would have been called to account and as the scriptures declare:

"You shall break them [the nations] with a rod of iron and dash them in pieces like a potter's vessel."" (Ps. 2:9)

"He will execute judgment among the nations, filling them with corpses; he will shatter chiefs over the wide earth. He will drink from the brook by the way; therefore he will lift up his head." (Ps. 110:6–7)

If Israel could have accepted their own Messiah to rule over them, if they could have recognized the day of their visitation, it would have been glorious for the nation of Israel but for the nations, only the fearful expectation of judgment.

If Israel did not reject their king and hand Him over to the Romans for execution Yeshua could have still fulfilled His kingly role but He would have not fulfilled His role as priest. He would not have been given over as *"The Lamb of God who takes away the sin of the world."* The nations would still be *"separated from Christ, alienated from the commonwealth of Israel and strangers to the covenants of promise, having no hope and without God in the world"* (Eph. 2:12). Of course, this is all speculative fancy because as representatives of sinful humanity, sinful Israel would not, and I dare say, could not recognize the day of their visitation.

Israel was chosen, but like all the other nations of the world Israel was a sinful nation. Would any other nation, if they had been the chosen nation instead of Israel succeeded where Israel failed? Israel is the chosen nation but Israel is as sinful as the rest of humanity, and therefore as the chosen nation they have suffered consequences that the rest of humanity has not had to bear.

Therefore, the offence that grates against the truth that we are all beloved of God is no offence at all. Israel's chosenness was always for the sake of the nations and the nations are the beneficiaries of Israel's chosenness. Would the blessings conferred to Abraham have come to the nations without Israel? Would the scriptures, the Word of God? Would the nations have received this unspeakable treasure without Israel? And what of the greatest treasure, Yeshua the Messiah? Would the nations have received eternal life in him if there had been no Israel through whom he came into the world?

As Paul wrote, *"through their trespass salvation has come to the Gentiles"* (Rom. 11:11). Should not the nations be grateful that Israel was the chosen nation that has born the cost of that chosenness, suffered the consequences and as a result opened the way of salvation for the Gentiles? When one understands what Israel's chosenness is about there is no place for envy. One comes to understand that Israel's chosenness is not the legitimate offence against the dignity and worth of all people. It is blessing yes, but also a heavy burden. Envy is replaced with gratitude for a nation chosen of behalf of all people.

But there is another dimension of offence at Israel's chosenness. This does not offend against the good and the truth but against the darkness that dwells in the human heart. It is the same offence that Cain harboured, that Ishmael had, that provoked Esau to want to kill his brother Jacob. There is a potential in all people, believers included, for envy and resentment. And in the case of offence against the Jewish people there can be a spiritual component, even a demonic influence that preys upon the minds of good people, and a subtle resentment that hides just under the surface of our consciousness. David asked *"Search me, O God, and know my heart; Try me, and know my anxieties; and see if there is any wicked way in me, and lead me in the way everlasting"* (Ps. 139:23–24).

My friends and I wrote this to help others understand the significance and blessing of Israel's chosenness. But, sometimes, even sincere believers can have anti-Semitism operating in their souls, perhaps without them being aware that this is so. Whenever we consider the topic of Israel's chosenness, it is necessary for us to come before the Lord like David and ask if there is this anti-Semitic, wicked way in us. This is crucial, because if this is hindering our understanding we will miss the call of the Gentiles towards Israel and the Jewish people. We will not be able to truly grasp the significance of Paul's call to the Gentiles on Israel's behalf. The next chapter deals specifically with this calling as Paul outlined it in the Book of Romans. If we harbour resentment and envy, even if it is a subtle, subconscious enmity we will be hindered from embracing the call on the Gentiles as it relates to the power of God for salvation, to the Jew first...

Response: Jewish Chosenness and the Green Eyed Monster

Ernie Culley, Pastor, Ahava Life Center

Ernie Culley has been in ministry for over forty years. He has been a cross-cultural missionary, Bible college instructor and a pastor of several churches in the United States and Canada. Ernie and his wife Merrilyn pastor an urban church in Vancouver, British Columbia, Canada. (MS)

I've been a born again, charismatic Christian for 47 years. I've graduated from two Bible Colleges, hold a Bachelors Degree in Theology, and have done postgraduate studies. Along the way, the predominant view I was taught of the relationship between Israel and the Church, and subsequently, the view I regrettably taught to my students, was that Israel, through disobedience, had forfeited their blessings promised in the covenants and the Church had now inherited them. The scriptures regarding the return of Israel to their land had been fulfilled in the return from Babylon under Ezra and Nehemiah. The restoration promises in the scriptures no longer had any present application to Israel or the Jewish people; they had all been spiritually transferred to the Church. For many years that scenario was satisfactory to me. Then I made several trips to Israel, and fell in love with the land.

I began to reexamine the scriptures relevant to the restoration of Israel, and noticed many scriptures that indicated God would bring the descendants of Abraham, Isaac, and Jacob back from all the countries where they had been scattered. It dawned on me that Babylon was one country, situated in one direction relative to Israel. Suddenly those scriptures no longer fit the model I had been taught.

The more I read the scriptures, the more I realized that there were a multitude of prophesies that were in the process of being fulfilled right now, on our watch! I was convinced by the preponderance of Biblical evidence, that HaShem has indeed remembered His covenants and is regathering His ancient people to their land — now! I have heard it said, "The Bible does not need to be rewritten, but it does need to be reread." I agree.

Along life's journey I bumped up against some teachings in psychology. One of the topics I recall had to do with what the experts called, "The illusion of central position." It works like this: A baby is born, and from its first moments of existence outside the womb, every single piece of life experience teaches, and reaffirms, that the baby is the absolute centre of the universe. The child's vision is filled with the adoring faces of adults, the parents especially, hovering over the crib, seeking to minister to every real or imagined need or desire. Each and every moment is filled with mounting evidence that his is an accurate and balanced view of the entire world around him.

This delightful bit of self-delusion often persists until the inexpressible trauma of the introduction of a new sibling, or some other shattering change of course that deposits the nagging concept that maybe the original premise is inaccurate. What a profound shock to discover that his or her position of centrality in the universe must somehow share all the now treasured attention with another being.

The same psychology study moved on to the concept that the process of maturation was nothing less than the systematic dismantling of the "The illusion of central position." As more and more individuals and ideas encroach upon a rapidly eroding grasping for preeminence, there is a natural inclination to rage against the darkness. We want our central position, and we want it now!

Within a world of participation trophies, and an educational environment seemingly more set upon creating and maintaining the lofty goal of "self esteem" over any actual academic achievement, we launch into adolescence and then adulthood with a deep longing for our lost position.

Enter a theological construct of the God of the Bible actually having a chosen people. And insult of all insults, it isn't us! And we find ourselves hurtling headlong into the sin of envy.

I was well into my 50's, having been involved in active pulpit ministry for over 30 years before I ever heard my first sermon devoted to the subject of envy. That is an astonishing admission, given what James has to say on the subject of envy: *"For where envy and self-seeking exist, confusion and every evil thing are there"* (James 3:16 NKJV). Did you get that? That is as profound and all embracing a scripture as, *"For the love of money is a root of all kinds of evil"* (1 Tim. 6:10 NKJV).

Why haven't we heard more about envy? James warns us that envy opens the door to every imaginable sort of evil!

Envy was the principal motivation of the religious leaders of Yeshua's day that led to their desire to kill him, and envy is killing the Body of Messiah to this day.

Envy differs from jealousy in that jealousy says, "Don't you dare touch what us mine!" while envy says, "I am going to take what is yours!" Envy springs from dissatisfaction with what we have been given, and a desire to grab another's gift.

Applying these thoughts to the subject at hand, upon hearing that our loving God has chosen someone other than ourselves as a special people, singled out for special purpose, then any uncrucified Illusion of central position, any unrepentant envy, and any of us can become prime candidates to descend into the pit of Anti-Semitism.

For help and remedy, we turn to no one less than Yeshua Himself. There is an account in the Gospels of the Last Supper where He did a bewildering thing:

> *"Jesus, knowing that the Father had given all things into his hands, and that he had come from God and was going back to God, rose from supper. He laid aside his outer garments, and taking a towel, tied it around his waist. Then he poured water into a basin and began to wash the disciples' feet and to wipe them with the towel that was wrapped around him."*
> (John 13:3-5)

The idea here is that Yeshua knew where He came from, knew where He was going, and was completely stable and secure in His identity. Therefore, from that platform, He could step into a role of complete humility and adopt the most subservient role of the lowliest domestic servant.

When we become so well grounded in our identity, gone will be the desire or necessity to defend our exalted illusion of central position. Instead we will be free to rejoice in another's gifting or calling, knowing that we too have been chosen, for our own position of function, honour, and blessing by the very same God. Together we take our rightful place in His Divine Kingdom, fulfilling our role that is unique to ourselves, and experiencing maximum deep fulfillment.

No longer will we be the little children in the sandbox, grabbing another child's treasured toy, and crying, "mine!" Slain will be the Green Eyed Monster of Envy!

CHAPTER 5

Romans: The Expanded Explanation of the Mystery

In his letter to the Galatians, Paul explains that he received his gospel by way of revelation and was commissioned to take this gospel to the Gentiles. Paul does so to establish his authority to correct the Galatians in their misguided belief that as Gentiles, they were required to come under Torah observance as if they were Jews.

When we reflect on Paul's very strong opposition to Gentiles seeking to observe Torah as Jews it is important to remember that Paul himself was a Torah observant Jew. In Acts 21, we have Luke's account of Paul's fourth visit to the church in Jerusalem.[26] Paul's visit arouses controversy among the believers, James (Yakov) explains:

> *You see, brother, how many thousands there are among the Jews of those who have believed. They are all zealous for the law, and they have been told about*

---

[26] Acts 9:26; 15:2; 18:21,22; 21:17ff - As per Paul's narrative in Galatians there may have been other occasions when he reported to the Jerusalem church (see, Gal. 1:18 - 2:2).

you that you teach all the Jews who are among the
Gentiles to forsake Moses, telling them not to Gentiles
to forsake Moses, telling them not to circumcise their
children or walk according to our customs."
(Acts 21:20–21)

A cursory review of Paul's letter to the Galatians might give the impression that Paul was in fact teaching Jews to "forsake Moses." The key distinction is that those Jewish believers who were suspicious of Paul were accusing him of teaching Jews living in the diaspora to abandon circumcision and Torah observance. When we recognize that Galatians is written to Gentile believers [27] we understand that this accusation was baseless. In order to remove all doubt as to where Paul stood, Yakov suggests Paul participate in a public act of Torah observance:

> *"Do therefore what we tell you. We have four men*
> *who are under a vow; take these men and purify*
> *yourself along with them and pay their expenses, so*
> *that they may shave their heads."* (Acts 21:23–24)

Paul willingly submits to Yakov [*James*] in order to assure the Jerusalem congregation that he has not forsaken his own Torah observance. As Yakov explained, *"All will know that there is nothing in what they have been told about you, but that you yourself also live in observance of the law"* (Acts 21:24). However, with respect to the Gentiles, both Paul and Yakov agreed:

---

[27] Gal. 1:16; 3:7; 4:8; 5:2

"But as for the Gentiles who have believed, we have sent a letter with our judgment that they should abstain from what has been sacrificed to idols, and from blood, and from what has been strangled, and from sexual immorality" (Acts 21:25).

Here Yakov is referring to the decision of what is commonly known as the Jerusalem Council - the first council of the church to establish a doctrinal precedent for all believers. The council's judgment was that Gentiles did not need to first convert to Judaism in order to follow Yeshua. Of course, the fact that the Jerusalem church had to convene a council on this issue infers that the Jewish church in Jerusalem understood that as Jews they were to continue a Torah observant life. If they themselves no longer observed the Torah there would have been no reason to convene a council to determine whether Gentiles should be required to do so.[28]

The council's decision is another example of the distinction between Jews and Gentiles, even among those who share oneness as followers of Messiah. Paul comments on this distinctiveness in the first chapter of his letter to the Romans by declaring that the gospel is *"to the Jew first and also to the Greek"* (Ro 1:16). Why did Paul add these words? Why didn't he just finish his testimony the way most of us usually quote this verse, that is, ending with *"to everyone who believes"*? If there were no distinction between how the gospel is directed to Jews and Gentiles then a declaration of the power of God to

---

[28] For an excellent discussion of this issue see, Kinzer, Mark S. *Postmissionary Messianic Judaism* (Grand Rapids, MI: Brazos Press 2005) 151-179

Paul - to Gentiles   Peter - to Jews

salvation for every believer would have sufficed. But Paul adds this curious distinction, *"to the Jew first, and also to the Greek."*

Paul was the apostle commissioned to take the gospel to the Gentiles, the apostles before him recognized this commission just as they also understood Peter was called to take the gospel to the Jewish people (Gal. 2:7,8). Paul's letter to the Romans is directed to Gentile believers (Rom. 1:13-15) and yet at the beginning of his letter he wants these Gentile believers to understand there is a certain priority regarding the gospel and the Jewish people. This is not just to contrast what he had said earlier about his obligation to *"Greeks and barbarians"* (Rom. 1:15). Paul wanted his Gentile audience in Rome to understand this distinction because it had everything to do with the gospel to the Gentiles and their call to the Jewish people.

Unlike Galatians, Paul's letter to the Romans is not primarily a response to doctrinal error or as the case with the Corinthians, a correction of moral failure. *Paul* He had not planted the Roman church and he only knew them by reputation.[29] One could say this letter was Paul's calling card, letting the Romans know the message he intended to preach to them when he finally was able to visit them in person.[30] Paul ends this letter describing its contents as *"my gospel"* (Rom. 16:25).

---

[29] Paul knew a few individuals in Rome – most notably his fellow Jewish workers among the Gentiles, Aquila and Priscilla (Rom. 16:3-15)

[30] Commentators over the years have suggested many alternative reasons for Paul's purpose in writing this letter. Leon Morris cites 11 different views before settling on the most straightforward reason: Paul wrote the letter as an introduction, on occasion of preparing the Roman church for his upcoming visit.

Leon Morris. "The Epistle to the Romans" (Grand Rapids, MI: Eerdmans, 1988) 7-18

One could say that this masterful book so well known a̶ revered by Christians through the ages is an exposition of t̶h̶e̶ gospel Paul received by revelation in the Arabian Desert. It is his theology, his gospel, and it has everything to do with the mystery of Israel, the calling of the Gentiles to the Jewish people and the priority of the gospel to the Jew first.

What does *"to the Jew first"* mean? As I wrote in the prologue most commentators understand this to be an issue of chronology not priority. That is, the gospel went to the Jews first, before it went to the Gentiles. It is true, that even Paul, the apostle to the Gentiles, when he came into a new town sought out the Jews first before he preached to the Gentiles. But even the gospel to the Jews first in chronology indicates a certain first in priority. For example, the guest of honour is served "first". However, I do not believe the "first" Paul had in mine is solely an issue of chronology.

The gospel to the Jew first, especially as it relates to the gospel to the Gentiles, is an issue of priority because the salvation of the Jewish people is a high priority calling for the Gentile church. That may seem like a radical, even unbalanced view but only because we have neglected this priority. This failure to recognize the calling of the Gentile believers towards the Jewish people is because the Church embraced the error that the Gentile church had replaced Israel as the people of God. Paul goes to great lengths in the Book of Romans to warn the Gentiles against this error.

Paul extends this warning as a caution against arrogance towards the Jewish people. Paul warns the Gentiles not to boast against the Jewish domestic olive branches that were broken off so that Gentile wild branches could be grafted on.

123

After all, the Olive tree represents Israel (Rom. 11:24) and as Paul notes, how can a branch boast against the root? The root supports the branch, not the other way around (Rom. 11:19).[31]

Paul goes a step further. He explains that Israel's failure to recognize their own Messiah was the condition that allowed the Gentiles into God's family:

> *"So I ask, did they stumble in order that they might fall? By no means! Rather through their trespass salvation has come to the Gentiles."* (Rom. 11:11)

Paul echoes this same turn of events in Romans 11:15: *"their rejection means the reconciliation of the world,"* and Romans 11:19: *"you will say, 'Branches were broken off so that I might be grafted in.'"*

The relationship of benefit for Gentiles is directly inverse to the outcome for Israel: Israel's trespass = Gentile salvation, Israel's rejection = Gentile reconciliation, Israel's branches broken off = Gentile branches grafted in. An awareness of the misfortune for one that brought such great bounty to others should erase any consideration of boasting. Rather, the appropriate posture would be gratitude and pity for the Jewish misfortune that resulted in Gentile blessing.

---

[31] The image of Israel as the olive tree whose branches were broken off is a reference to Jeremiah 11:16: *"The LORD called your name, Green Olive Tree, lovely and of good fruit. With the noise of a great tumult He has kindled fire on it, and its branches are broken."*

This image of Gentiles being grafted into Israel is similar in function to the image breaking down of the wall of partition excluding Gentiles from Israel's status as God's people. In both images the Gentiles join Israel so as to enjoy Israel's privileges as the people of God.

This fall of the one is for the benefit of the other; this salvation that came to the Gentiles by way of Israel's failure was conceived in the plan of God and has tremendous significance for both Jews and Gentiles. Can there be any animosity from Gentile believers towards the Jewish people if Jewish misfortune is directly responsible for Gentile salvation? God's election of Israel as His chosen people was determined with the benefit of the foresight that knew Israel would fail and in doing so, open access for the Gentiles into God's family as the people of God. One could easily make the case that Israel's choseness was ultimately for the sake of the Gentiles.

So far this relationship appears to be heavily one sided, as I mentioned earlier, in any good relationship blessings and responsibilities must flow both ways. What appeared to be exclusive Jewish benefit turned out to be quite the opposite. But has God now rejected the one in favour of the other? Have all the blessings that were Israel's sole domain now passed onto the Gentiles, leaving Israel deplete of blessing? Is Israel only left with failure, rejection and being broken off? Paul anticipates this question by asking hypothetically, *"So I ask, did they stumble in order that they might fall?"* (Rom. 11:11). His answer addresses the seeming disparity between Israel's fall and the Gentile salvation: *"By no means!*[32] *Rather through their trespass salvation has come to the Gentiles, so as to make Israel jealous"* (Rom. 11:11).

Romans 11:11 is startling, Paul is saying that salvation has come to the nations of the world for Israel's sake – to make

---

[32] μὴ γένοιτο (*mē genoito*) this is the most forceful "no" available in Greek. "By no means" is a good literal translation; "certainly not!" is a suitable English equivalent.

Israel jealous. This is the flip side of the much more familiar passage, John 3:16 which states salvation has come to Israel because God so loves the world that he gave His son for the sake of all. Romans 11:11 is not about God so loving the world, but God so loving Israel. The supreme gift of salvation is given to the Gentiles with an intention for the impact of this gift on Israel. I think one would be hard pressed to find any evangelistic sermon ever proclaiming salvation has come to the world to make Israel jealous – we simply do not look at salvation in terms of its impact on others, let alone on Israel. The Gospel message is almost always presented in terms of what it can do for us as individuals. This is not wrong, John 3:16 is just as authoritative as Romans 11:11. However, we cannot ignore the clear message of Romans 11:11 either. It behooves all Gentile Christians to consider that their salvation has a purpose beyond themselves, a purpose specifically for Israel. We should also ask what response to salvation is required of the Gentiles (if any), to ensure the purpose of making Israel jealous is actualized.

Instead of focusing on Israel's fall resulting in Gentile's salvation, Romans 11:11 shifts the benefit back to Israel. Gentile salvation is to provoke Israel to jealousy and thereby turn Israel's attention back to their Messiah. Does this mean that the Gentiles are no more than a tool in a spurned lover's hand, used to attract his wayward object of affection? The next verse restores the balance of mutual blessing between Israel and the nations.

"Now if their fall is riches for the world, and their failure riches for the Gentiles, how much more their fullness!" (Rom. 11:12)

Paul presents a scenario to the Gentiles in Rome that should compel them to get on with the job of provoking Israel to jealousy. He asks them to consider just how much Israel's fall has meant for the Gentiles and consider how much greater blessings (Paul uses the term "riches"), would come to the Gentiles on account of Israel's restoration. God's purposes are always restorative, Israel has not stumbled so as to fall beyond recovery, Paul is asking the Romans to imagine that if their failure and fall resulted in such great, rich blessings to the world, how much more benefit Israel's restoration would be to those same Gentiles, who received so much on account of Israel's fall.

Verse 13 reiterates that this is a message for the Gentiles from the apostle commissioned to preach the gospel to the Gentiles: *"Now I am speaking to you Gentiles. Inasmuch then as I am an apostle to the Gentiles, I magnify my ministry"* (Rom. 11:13). This is the message of the gospel that is unique to the Gentiles that Peter was not preaching to the Jews. This is the dimension of salvation that is a message for Gentiles because it is a call exclusive to the Gentiles on Israel's behalf. To be clear, Israel always had a call on behalf of the Gentiles, but now the call is extended to the Gentiles to ensure the blessings flow in both directions – the Gentiles blessing Israel and Israel blessing the Gentiles. The two calls are symbiotic; as the Gentiles provoke Israel to jealousy, and thereby contribute to Israel's restoration (Israel's blessing), so the Gentiles will receive greater riches then they had already received on account of Israel's fall (Gentile's blessing). Paul explains, *"For if their being cast away is the reconciling of the world, what will their acceptance be but life from the dead?"* (Rom. 11:15).

When will this resurrection occur? Paul is again instructing the Gentiles to not be ignorant of the mystery of Israel's fallen condition.

"For I do not desire, brethren, that you should be ignorant of this mystery, lest you should be wise in your own opinion, that blindness in part has happened to Israel until the fullness of the Gentiles has come in." (Rom. 11:25)

This is so important for the church today. Ignorance of the mystery of Israel produces grace-resisting arrogance (See, 1 Pet. 5:5; Pr. 3:34). Earlier Paul warned the Romans *"do not boast against the branches... Do not be haughty, but fear"* (Rom. 11:18,19). The idea that God has rejected Israel or that Israel is no longer necessary in the plan of God smacks of what Paul called boasting against the branches (Rom. 11:18). How much grace has been restricted from being poured out upon the church because of this arrogance? To what extent have the greater riches for the world been delayed by the Church's failure to understand this mystery?

My intention is not to scold, but to encourage us all to understand the mystery, the call and the reward. A great resurrection that produces untold blessing is still to come, but it will not happen until the church awakens to their call to

Israel, until every vestige of the arrogance inducing replacement perspective is repudiated and renounced.

Romans 11:25 tells us that Israel's blindness (please note, it is a partial not complete blindness) is temporary. Illumination is dependent on the Gentiles coming into their fullness. A number of English translations translate the Greek word for fullness as "full number." This gives the impression that Israel's illumination is dependent on a certain number of Gentiles coming to salvation. There is nothing of Gentile call in view, rather there is a number chosen by the Father, that once reached, releases favour on Israel. I think this translation reflects a certain theological bias that removes Gentile calling towards Israel. The same Greek word[33] is used to describe Israel's restoration in Romans 11:12. Here Paul is clearly not speaking of a certain number of Jews who are restored in order to release greater riches to the world.

In chapter 11, Paul is contrasting the benefit of Israel's fullness for the Gentiles (greater riches, v. 12), with the benefit of Gentile fullness for Israel (removal of partial blindness v.25). The whole chapter addresses the connection between Israel and the Gentiles, it seems unnecessary to me to change the meaning of the word understood in verse 12 (Israel's qualitative fullness), when considering the content of verse 25 (the fullness of the Gentiles). The context of contrast between Israel's fullness and Gentile fullness argues for parallel meaning. Romans 11:25 also stresses Gentile calling to Israel (I will

---

[33] πλήρωμα (plērōma) can be translated as fullness or full number. The translators had to choose either option based on context and theological understanding. As above, I think the context and theology dictate that "fullness" is the correct choice. This is how the translators of the ESV, KJV, NKJV, and NASB render pleroma.

address this further below), so the theology of the passage also supports the idea of Gentile fullness being in view rather than a full number of Gentiles being realized.

If we are waiting for a certain number of Gentiles to be saved before Israel is restored then the only responsibility the Gentiles have towards Israel is to evangelize other Gentiles. This theology does not account for God's purposes of mutual call and mutual blessing. It does not account for God's purpose to make One New Man out of the two. Paul goes on to assure the Romans that Israel's restoration is guaranteed because *"the gifts and the calling of God are irrevocable"* (Rom. 11:29). But if this restoration is connected to the Gentiles reaching their fullness, and this fullness is connected to the Gentiles not being ignorant of the mystery of Israel, then it is crucial for the Gentile church to understand how their call to provoke Israel to jealousy contributes towards the Gentiles reaching their own fullness. The call to provoke Israel to jealousy and the expectation of the Gentile church entering into its fullness for the sake of Israel's illumination are two sides of the same coin.

The last section of Paul's discourse in Romans regarding the relationship between Jews and Gentiles connects the Gentiles achieving their fullness and their call to provoke Israel to Jealousy together. In Romans 11:30-32, Paul explains how the Gentiles are to come into their fullness through their salvation based call to minister to Israel.

"For just as you were at one time disobedient to God but now have received mercy because of their disobedience, so they too have now been disobedient in order that by the mercy shown to you they also may

now receive mercy. For God has consigned all to disobedience, that he may have mercy on all." (Rom. 11:30–32)

This is the apex of the Letter to the Romans, what Paul had been building towards since the first chapter when he declared the gospel unto salvation is for the Jew first and also to the Greek. Paul reminds the Roman Gentiles of their former condition, *"You [Gentiles] were at one time disobedient to God"* (Rom. 11:30a), but now have become the recipients of mercy *"because of their [Israel's] disobedience"* (Rom. 11:30b). Paul is repeating what he had already written earlier in the chapter, Jewish failure meant Gentile salvation (Rom. 11:11), Jewish casting away meant Gentile reconciliation (Rom. 11:15), and Jewish branches broken off meant Gentile branches grafted in (Rom. 11:19).

The relationship between the two realities for Jews and Gentiles may seem difficult to connect. How does disobedience of the one result in mercy for the other? Let's consider again what would have taken place had Israel recognized *"the time of their visitation"* (Luke 19:44). If, when Yeshua entered Jerusalem on a donkey's foal the leaders of the nation, instead of rejecting him and delivering him to the Romans for execution would have yielded to him as their king and worshipped him as their Lord, Yeshua would have rightfully taken the throne of his father David and ruled over the House of Jacob forever.[34]

---

[34] See, Luke 1:33. Of course, Yeshua does rule over Israel as King.

But what of the Gentiles? They would have still been in their former condition, strangers to the covenants, without hope and without God (Eph. 2:12). It is because Israel failed to recognize their king that he was given over as *"the Lamb of God who takes away the sin of the world"* (John 1:29). This is what Paul is describing in Romans 11:30. Israel's disobedience meant mercy for the Gentiles. The Gentiles were at one time by nature all disobedient (Eph. 2:2), but now through the blood of the Messiah those Gentiles who put their trust in him receive mercy because they come under Yeshua's atoning sacrifice. Paul is saying this could not have happened without Israel first being disobedient.

In God's plan of salvation for the whole world, His elect people Israel had to fail to recognize the day of their visitation from their own Messiah. Gentiles, who were by nature disobedient, were now the recipients of mercy and Israel; the elect people of God had now become disobedient in need of mercy. What a role reversal! How does Israel again obtain mercy?

> *"For just as you were at one time disobedient to God but now have received mercy because of their disobedience, so they too have now been disobedient in order that by the mercy shown to you they also may now receive mercy.* (Rom. 11:30–31)

Disobedient Israel obtains mercy by receiving mercy from the Gentiles. It was ultimately for the sake of the Gentiles that Israel was "consigned" to disobedience in order that the Gentiles could obtain mercy. God established this pattern in which He *"has consigned all to disobedience, that he may have mercy on all"* (Rom. 11:32). There is no favourite; there is no one obedient, no one without the need for mercy. As Paul wrote earlier *"All [Jews and Gentiles] have sinned and fall short of the glory of God"* (Rom. 3:23). But this is so God in Messiah can show mercy to both Jews and Gentiles.

In the same way that the Gentiles could not have received mercy without Israel's disobedience, so now Israel cannot receive mercy without Gentile obedience to show Israel mercy.

This is the call of the Gentiles to Israel as explained by the apostle to the Gentiles. Paul the Jew, who was willing to suffer eternal condemnation for the sake of Israel (Rom. 9:3), makes his appeal to the Gentiles to show mercy to his own people. He reminds them that they would have never received mercy if it were not for Israel's disobedience. Yes, as the scriptures promise, *"All Israel shall be saved"* (Rom. 11:26). But this is not a work apart from the Gentiles, it comes to pass as the Gentiles enter into their fullness and show mercy back to Israel for the mercy they received. The immensity, beauty and wisdom of this plan of salvation forces Paul to pause his exhortation to worship the only wise God:

> *"Oh, the depth of the riches and wisdom and knowledge of God! How unsearchable are his judgments and how inscrutable his ways! "For who has known the mind of the Lord, or who has been his counselor?" "Or who has given a gift to him that he might be repaid?" For from him and through him and to him are all things. To him be glory forever. Amen."* (Rom. 11:33–36)

When Paul considers how in His wisdom, God so ordered salvation for both Jews and Gentiles in such a way that neither could boast, that disobedient Israel and disobedient Gentiles both receive mercy from each other and that both would need each other to complete the plan, all Paul can do is worship. This awesome plan is ultimately not about Israel or the Gentiles; it is all *"from Him, through Him and to Him."* Only to God can glory be ascribed. I add my hearty "Amen!"

Now Paul returns to the exhortation:

> *"I appeal to you therefore, brothers, by the mercies of God, to present your bodies as a living sacrifice, holy and acceptable to God, which is your spiritual worship. Do not be conformed to this world, but be transformed by the renewal of your mind, that by testing you may discern what is the will of God, what is good and acceptable and perfect."* (Rom. 12:1–2)

When Paul wrote his letter to the Romans he did not include chapter headings and verse notation. We have been beguiled in part by our reliance on these chapter and verse divisions into breaking up Paul's argument in line with these chapter breaks. The mystery of Israel and the call of the Gentiles to Israel do not end with the completion of Romans chapter 11. Romans 12 begins with an appeal to the Gentiles in Rome on account of God's mercy. That is, the mercy they received on account of Israel's disobedience in order that they would now extend mercy back to Israel. This is the "therefore" mercy in view that should therefore compel the Romans to present their bodies as living sacrifices.

How many sermons have been preached on Romans 12:1,2? How many point back to the mercy the Gentiles received as explained in Romans 11? I dare say, hardly any. Yet, if we follow the exhortation in Romans 11, there is not doubt that this is the "therefore mercy" referred to by Paul. Romans 12:1,2 is perhaps the strongest call to the believer's sanctification. Of course, it is a call because of God's grace, mercy, love and deliverance from the bondage of sin as outlined by Paul earlier in Romans, but specifically, the context is the mercy received on account of Israel's disobedience in order to extend mercy back to Israel. This is no minor side issue. This is not the unique call of the "Israel lovers" in our local churches. This is the mandate of the church among the Gentiles. It is the basis for laying down ones life and yielding ones will completely in submission to God as a living sacrifice.

The outcome of this yielding to this call is no less than transformation. It is the radical shift in thinking through a mind renewed in line with the mind of the Messiah. It is obtaining the discernment to know what God's will is, it is everything we long for regarding our spiritual growth and maturity, it is coming into our fullness. So much encouraging and helpful insights has been taught on Romans 12:1-2. If we truly live our lives according to this exhortation we will move in dimensions of love, authority and wisdom that bear powerful witness to the truth of the gospel and the claims of Yeshua the Messiah.

Please consider, we will never truly obey the call to lay our lives down as living sacrifices if we do not address the first purpose for this sanctification: showing mercy to Israel. God forgive us for ignoring this vital dimension of the message. It is time for Yeshua's church in the nations to take this call seriously and repent for dismissing it as no longer relevant or a fringe issue for a just a few. Salvation was given to the Gentiles in order to make Israel jealous and the Gentiles are called to lay their lives down as living sacrifices to show mercy back to Israel. This is no small thing. It is the catalyst that propels both Jews and Gentiles into their fullness. The result is the end of spiritual blindness for Israel and lavish riches bestowed on the nations such as they have never seen.

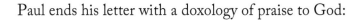

Paul ends his letter with a doxology of praise to God:

> *"Now to him who is able to strengthen you according to my gospel and the preaching of Jesus Christ, according to the revelation of the mystery that was kept secret for long ages but has now been disclosed and through the prophetic writings has been made known to all nations, according to the command of the eternal God, to bring about the obedience of faith."* (Rom. 16:25–26)

God is the one who is well able to strengthen the believers in Rome with the ultimate end of obedience to the faith. In chapter one Paul declares he is not ashamed of the gospel; here Paul sums up his explanation of the gospel in his letter to the Romans by stating this gospel is "his" gospel. The gospel he received as a revelation of a mystery that heretofore had been a secret but now had been revealed to the apostle. This secret, long kept hidden had been hidden in plain sight because it was disclosed *"through the prophetic writings"*.

This is not a reference to new prophetic revelation, but the prophetic writings recorded in the Hebrew Scriptures.[35] This is a reiteration of what Paul wrote in in his opening chapter. In his introduction, he explained that he was an apostle *"set apart for the gospel of God, which he promised beforehand through the prophets in the Holy Scriptures"* (Rom. 1:1,2). Paul's revelation is not something completely new without connection back to God's original plan and purpose.

This new revelation is a clarification and expansion of the original plan and purpose of God as set out in the Hebrew Scriptures. A plan to chose Israel on behalf of all the nations. What is startlingly new is that this plan also includes the nations showing mercy to Israel. What is new is that this plan is now revealed to the nations in order that those who were by nature disobedient will embrace their call in Messiah to *"bring about obedience of faith."*

For most of church history the International Body of Messiah has been ignorant of the mystery of Israel and how that mystery is wrapped up in the mystery of the gospel, especially as it has been revealed to Paul, the Apostle to the Gentiles. Despite this poor track record, the good news is that it is God Himself who is the one who can strengthen us all for this task.

---

[35] Many commentators agree that here Paul is referring to the Hebrew Scriptures as represented by the prophets (see Rom. 3:21). Paul sites many references to the prophets in his letter to the Romans.

Our disobedience can be turned around to obedience. Our failure to grasp the mystery and thereby putting us at risk to grace-resisting arrogance can also be turned around by the transformation accomplished within us by the renewing of our minds. But first, we must respond to God's mercy to us in Messiah Yeshua by laying down our lives as living sacrifices. Today, the ancient call rings out to us as it did to Israel two millennia ago: *"The time is fulfilled, and the kingdom of God is at hand; repent and believe in the gospel"* (Mark 1:15).

POSTSCRIPT:

Israel's Blindness

I would like to return to the issue of Israel's blindness. Israel has been blinded. The blindness ends when the Church among the nations comes into its fullness (Rom. 11:25). Earlier in Romans 11, Paul addressed the issue of Israel's blindness:

> *"What then? Israel failed to obtain what it was seeking. The elect obtained it, but the rest were hardened, as it is written, 'God gave them a spirit of stupor, eyes that would not see and ears that would not hear, down to this very day.'"* (Rom. 11:7–8)

The *"as it is written"* quote is a conflation of two verses, Isaiah 29:10 and Deuteronomy 29:4. The Deuteronomy quote is very significant. The whole book of Deuteronomy is a re-telling of the Exodus and Israel's forty years of wilderness wanderings. Towards the end of the book Moses tells the people:

> *"And Moses summoned all Israel and said to them: You have seen all that the LORD did before your eyes in the land of Egypt, to Pharaoh and to all his servants and to all his land, the great trials that your eyes saw, the signs, and those great wonders. But to*

this day the LORD has not given you a heart to understand or eyes to see or ears to hear.'"
(Deut. 29:2–4)

Moses is perplexed. Israel has seen the awesome wonders of God. The scope and scale of HaShem's miraculous intervention had been demonstrated on an unprecedented scale — even to the present day. No nation before or since has seen such a miraculous demonstration of divine power. And yet for some reason that Moses could not understand, Israel was not given *"a heart to understand or eyes to see or ears to hear."* How after forty years of seeing manna every day, of never having to make new sandals or sew new clothes, of seeing the pillar of cloud by day and of fire by night could Israel still not see? When I read these words I sense Moses' frustration over this predicament. Forty years! Forty years!

Forty years is a blink of an eye compared to how long Israel has been waiting to see; not forty, not four hundred but almost thirty-five hundred years! The point is, as a nation Israel does not see until the Gentiles enter into their fullness. As a representative of the remnant of Israel saved by grace, can I please implore you dear Gentile brothers and sisters. Please enter into your fullness, embrace your call. We have been waiting such a long time for you. Not only will we finally get to see, but also you will receive the greater riches you have been longing for.

Wild branches grafted in

Paul uses the metaphor of the olive tree to give the Roman church a visual representation of God's judgment on Israel (the natural/domestic branches) and His saving acts on behalf of the Gentiles (the wild olive branches). That is, natural branches were broken off (Rom. 11:17-20), and wild branches were grafted in. Paul's analogy on the olive tree is the grounds for his admonition to Gentiles not to boast against the natural branches broken off. Gentiles are described as wild olive branches. Unbelieving Jews, as natural branches broken off but the tree itself is Israel. Paul makes this clear in Rom.11:24 where he speaks of natural branches grafted back into *"their own olive tree."* The metaphor of Israel as an olive tree with branches broken is originally found in Jeremiah 11.

> *"The LORD once called you 'a green olive tree, beautiful with good fruit.' But with the roar of a great tempest he will set fire to it, and its branches will be consumed."* (Jer. 11:16)

Jeremiah 11 is an indictment against Judah for prolonged disobedience. Because Judah had turned its back on the covenant so God would bring judgment that could not be averted. What was once a fruitful tree had become worthless and fit for the fire. A good friend of mine runs his own tour company in Israel. On one occasion, as we drove past the olive groves of Upper Galilee he remarked that fire does not kill an olive tree, neither does cutting it down. The only way to kill an olive tree is to pull it up by the roots. Though God brought judgement on Judah for disobedience, His covenant faithfulness remained. Earlier, Jeremiah had promised not to make a *"full end" of the House of Judah"* (Jer. 5:18).[36] This is an echo of the covenant promise of Leviticus 26:

> *"Yet for all that, when they are in the land of their enemies, I will not spurn them, neither will I abhor them so as to destroy them utterly and break my covenant with them, for I am the LORD their God."*
> (Lev. 26:44)

Paul is drawing on Jeremiah's vision of Israel with branches destroyed in judgment to explain Israel's present condition. Like the Kingdom of Judah in Jeremiah's day, judgment had come for unbelief/disobedience. But the judgement that broke off branches does not destroy the tree. As Paul put it, they did not stumble in order that they might fall completely (Rom. 11:11).

But what of the Gentiles grafted in? Paul describes them as wild olive branches. This is not a complimentary picture. Wild branches produce wild fruit. Wild olives are of no benefit. One does not press oil out of wild olives. Some commentators have relied on anecdotal evidence that in in the

---

[36] Jeremiah 5:10 also speaks of branches. The metaphor here is branches of the grape vine. The verse reads, *"Go up through her vine rows and destroy, but make not a full end; strip away her branches, for they are not the LORD's."* (Jer. 5:10)

first century, olive farmers would sometimes graft a wild olive branch onto a domesticated tree to improve it hardiness.[37]

This is a delightful story but it misses the point. Paul is not extolling any virtue to the grafted wild olive branch. I am not convinced Paul was making reference to this supposed practice. He noted, grafting a wild branch onto a domesticated tree is *"contrary to nature."* (Rom. 11:24) The fact is, that a branch grafted onto a tree does not have an effect on the tree. It is the other way around - a branch by itself cannot produce fruit but graft it onto a tree and the nourishment of the tree invigorates the branch to bear fruit.

As Paul explained, *"It is not you [Gentiles] who support the root, but the root [Israel] that supports you"* (Rom. 11:18). Further, a grafted branch bears fruit after its own species. When a farmer grafts a Granny Smith apple onto a Macintosh apple tree, that branch still bears Granny Smith apples - it cannot produce Macintosh apples. Likewise, a wild olive branch grafted onto to a domesticated olive tree can still only produce wild olives. And yet, in Paul's analogy, contrary to nature wild branches produce fat, juicy, productive olives.

> *"And if some of the branches were broken off, and you, being a wild olive tree, were grafted in among them, and with them became a partaker of the root and fatness of the olive tree, do not boast against the*

---

[37] W.M. Ramsay. "The Expositor" Sixth series II (1905) as quoted by CEF Cranfield. *Romans, Volume II.* "The International Critical Commentary", Editors, JA Emerton, CEB Cranfield (Edinburgh: T&T Clarke, 1979) p.566

branches. But if you do boast, remember that you do not
support the root, but the root supports you."
(Rom. 11:17–18 NKJV)

The Greek construction of the phrase "root and fatness" is a bit awkward.[38] There is no "and" in the original language. "Fatness of the root" is probably better. I choose the NKJV translation because most modern translations do not include the word fat, which is the same Greek word for oil.[39] The image is not of sap running from the root to nourish a wild branch bearing wild fruit, but fatness or oil, transmitted to the wild olive branch by virtue of it connection into the root of the domestic tree. This is a beautiful picture of One New Man.

Wild olive branches, which by nature are unfruitful, become as fruitful as natural branches because they are connected to the same root that sustains them both. This is akin to what Paul said to the Gentile believers in Ephesus. The Gentiles *"were by nature, children of wrath"* (Eph. 2:3). One could say that by nature, they were unfruitful. But now in Messiah, the elemental nature of believers is transformed. Gentiles, who once were not children of God (Eph. 2:12), in Messiah are made equal citizens in Israel (Eph. 2:13). Their nature is transformed in Messiah so as to now become fruitful. The grafted in wild branch produces fruit just like the domestic branch.

---

[38] James D. G. Dunn. *Romans 9-16 "Word Biblical Commentary" Editors, Bruce W. Metzger, David A. Hubbard, Glenn W. Barker (Grand Rapids, MI: Zondervan) Vol. 38B, p.651*

[39] πιότητος *piotaytos, fat, oil, richness.* The Hebrew word, שמן *shemen* can also be used for fat or fatness (See, Gen. 27:28,29)

Response: The Gospel and Aliyah

Joe Campbell, Pastor at large, Return Ministries.

Joe Campbell's response references a recording of a teaching I gave in 2011 at a church in Kitchener, Ontario. I choose Joe to respond to the chapter on Romans because he is an excellent Bible teacher. I did not know the details of how my teaching had an impact on his own life and ministry, nor was this part of my consideration for asking Joe to contribute to this book. (MS)

Marty Shoub's explanation and exegesis of Romans 11 significantly altered the path of my life early in 2013. I had just completed a seven year contract as the National Director of Development with a Christian Jewish-focused ministry in Canada. I was actively seeking Yeshua's direction for the next chapter in my vocational ministry. I was drawn to the faith-based organization of Return Ministries located near Bright, Ontario. I was extremely impressed with the leadership and direction of this ministry under Dean Bye; it was actively engaged in supporting Israel and the Jewish people and it was centred on the mission of Aliyah. I loved the first part of this focus as I had just devoted seven years of my lifetime to a Christian Zionist ministry that like Return Ministries was devoted to supporting Israel. However, it was the second part of Return's focus concerning the importance of Aliyah with which I struggled.

To give a bit of background, I had graduated from the Royal Military College in Kinston, Ontario and I immediately entered into the Canadian Armed Forces flight program where I served on jets and helicopters for six years. I then transitioned to commercial airlines where I served as a pilot on DC-8 aircraft for seven years, flying mostly to Europe. It was at this stage of my life that I had a dramatic engagement with Yeshua/Jesus on a layover in Amsterdam, Holland. I considered myself an agnostic at the time, but everything changed for me and my wife following that encounter.

My Damascus road experience redirected my priorities completely in every area of life. It was only a matter of time until I yielded to my heart's desire to preach/teach the Scriptures concerning Jesus as Lord and Saviour. I entered theological seminary, obtained a Masters of Divinity degree and entered into pastoral ministry. After 27 years in pastoral ministry, serving as a senior pastor in three denominations, God had a new path for me. I loved the pastoral ministry, and I loved preaching salvation through Jesus Christ; I was neutral concerning Israel as a nation, but was supportive of the Jewish people.

And then I participated in a Watchmen For The Nations Gathering in Winnipeg, Manitoba in the summer of 1999. Everything concerning Israel changed for me and my wife following that three-day gathering. The Lord downloaded an overpowering love for Israel and the Jewish people, which greatly affected my pastoral ministry. I now was actively seeking ways to support, bless and pray for Israel and its people on a regular basis. In Winnipeg, I received the revelation and impartation of Father's incredible love for His chosen people. That 'imputed love' later led me to leaving the pastoral ministry to join a national Israel-focused ministry, as previously mentioned.

But back to my dilemma...I strongly sensed I was to become a part of Return Ministries; they had been praying for years for a person to serve in the ministry of teaching and pastoral care to interns and volunteers that lived on the Return base. My problem was that although I saw that Aliyah was alluded to in the prophetic Scriptures, I could not embrace Aliyah as central to the gospel. I could not commit myself to the ministry of Return until I had discovered this key. I knew that I was missing an important piece of the puzzle and I was not able to figure it out. I asked many questions and examined many Scriptures, but I just could not see how God's plan for Israel and the Church came together.

Then someone gave a teaching CD entitled, 'A Biblical Perspective on Israel'[40] taught by Marty Shoub. The teaching contained an explanation of Ezekiel 36, followed by Romans 11 and the 'One New Man' principle. It was like a light bulb went off inside my head. I finally saw God's plan. Marty began with a few comments about Aliyah in his CD teaching, and then transitioned into God's passion for seeing Gentiles complete His plan of provoking the Jews to jealousy. Suddenly, all the pieces came together and the mystery of the jigsaw puzzle in my mind was solved.

---

[40] This CD can be obtained through Return Ministries.

One after another, as Marty spoke, I saw truths that I had not seen previously. I saw that Paul had not become an apostle to the Gentiles because he had 'given up' on the Jewish people; he did so out of an intense and enduring love for the Jewish people. Paul saw that 'salvation to the Gentiles' was a strategic part of God's plan to reach his own people. And then I saw that the role of the Gentiles was clear…to provoke the Jews to jealousy so that the Jews would yearn for Messiah.

I was totally challenged by Marty's revelation concerning the 'fullness of the Gentiles'. I had previously understood this concept to be 'a certain number'. When I grasped the fact that the passage is speaking about God's purposes of 'mutual call and mutual blessing', suddenly I saw why Paul was linking verse 12 with verse 15 in Romans 11; each of us (Jews and Gentiles) have been called to mutually bring the other to receiving salvation! We each have a mutual call in God's amazing plan to bring salvation to each other…and to the whole world. We each have the task of blessing each other! My mind was imploding with thoughts concerning the immensity of the twin concepts of the coming effect on the Gentiles following the 'fullness' of the Jews (v.12), and the coming effect of 'life from the dead' for the Gentiles, following the 'acceptance' of the Jews (v.15).

Personally, I then saw salvation in a whole new light…that very salvation that I so loved to preach and teach for so many years. But now I realized that the Church must no longer leave Israel and the Jewish people out of the 'salvation picture'. I categorically knew I had to seek ways to 'provoke the Jews to jealousy'. Was it through unconditional love? Was it to let the light of Yeshua shine through me? Was it through signs and wonders in my ministry? These questions and many more flooded through my brain. However, one imperative I fully grasped at that time…I knew that it was imperative to assist in getting the Jews back to Israel where Yeshua would be revealed to them as a nation. I understood that Yeshua was about to reveal Himself to the Jews in Israel…as a nation.

I realized that their 'blindness in part' was as a nation, not simply as individuals. God was about bring a whole nation to a conversion experience. This has never happened before and it was being reserved for God's chosen people, the Jews. As Gentiles, we come to submission to the lordship of Yeshua individually…and it will continue to be that way until the end. However, the Jews are the only ones that will have the revelation and experience of salvation as a nation. And when that happens, God's Name will be sanctified/hallowed…and all the world will know that He is LORD!

Of course, this immediately caused me to realize the incredible importance of getting the Jews back to Israel. It involves the hallowing of the Name of the LORD, the salvation of the Jews and the amazing experience of *"life from the dead"* for the Gentiles (Rom. 11:15).

Suddenly, Isaiah 49:22 became paramount; as a Gentile believer, my role must include bringing the Jews back home 'in my arms' and 'on my shoulders'. I now saw Aliyah as central to the gospel of Jesus Christ. It was no longer peripheral, it was at the very centre…and I had missed it all these years of my ministry. I also understood the necessity of practicing the 'one new man' principle by becoming more connected with Messianic Jewish believers in worship, prayer and ministry. In my previous ministry position, we avoided direct Messianic connections and involvement. I had a new desire to learn more about my Messianic brothers and sisters. I began to seek new ways to implement this 'one new man' principle, which I had never embraced previously. Oh, how life has changed through one revelation download. Needless to say, I joined Return Ministries to serve in the role of teacher and pastoral care.

Presently, I am involved in five different ministries, with Return Ministries being my primary involvement. I remain connected to and involved with a church that loves and embraces Israel. As well, I am actively involved in a national inner healing ministry, which is based on 'ancient paths' principles (Jer. 6:16). Another area of ministry in which I am involved is one called, 'Stand On Guard Prayer'. As the leader of the Israel-focused part of this ministry, I lead Intercessors from across Canada in prayer for Israel for one hour each week via teleconference calls. It has been such a delight to impart to the Intercessors the concepts that Yeshua has illuminated, through Marty, to me.

How gratifying to see each week Intercessors release mercy through intercessory prayer to the Jewish people. How gratifying to see the concepts discussed in this chapter imparted to the many Christian interns and volunteers as they pass through Return Ministries and are trained to serve Jewish people with unconditional love.

At this point in my life, I desire to be a conduit of God's love and grace so that I might impact others in the Church to see and understand the mystery of the gospel of Jesus Christ...a mystery so often missed in most Christian churches in the western world. My desire is that anyone reading these remarks will likewise be impacted to see beyond the 'normal'

into the 'super-normal' of God's great plan for the future…
even the very *'restoration of all things'* (Acts 3:19-21).

CHAPTER 6

The Wealth of the Gentiles

"Lift up your eyes all around, and see; they all gather together, they come to you; your sons shall come from afar, and your daughters shall be carried on the hip. Then you shall see and be radiant; your heart shall thrill and exult, because the abundance of the sea shall be turned to you, the wealth of the nations shall come to you."
(Isa. 60:4–5)

Throughout the scriptures we find a curious pattern. HaShem's enterprises on Israel's behalf are funded by those from the nations. Even Abraham, whom HaShem promises to bless, receives much of his outstanding wealth from Gentile rulers. Consider Abraham's fearful deception, ordering Sarah to deny she was his wife, commanding her to only acknowledge that she was his sister.[41] In Genesis 12:16 we read *"And for her sake he [Pharaoh], dealt well with Abram; and he had sheep, oxen, male donkeys, male servants, female servants, female donkeys, and camels."* In a subtle way this verse is telling us that Abraham had sheep, oxen, donkeys, etc., because Pharaoh *"dealt well*

---

[41] According to Genesis 20:12 Sarah is Abraham's half sister. They had different mothers. This practice is later prohibited by Torah (Lev. 18:9).

with" Abraham - that is, Pharaoh gave Abraham all these things.[42] Later, Abraham repeats this deception on Abimelech, the Philistine king with the same results, amassing even more wealth (See, Gen. 20:1-14).

It may seem unfair. Abraham practices deceit, not once but twice. On both occasions he is blessed with extravagant material wealth and surely, not for any justifiable recompense. Despite his deceitfulness, HaShem blesses Abraham by the hand of Gentile rulers.

In Genesis 15 HaShem ratifies the covenant to bless Abraham with descendants and land by passing through the pieces as a burning torch. With this amazing demonstration of covenant fidelity [43] HaShem makes the following declaration:

> *"As the sun was going down, a deep sleep fell on Abram. And behold, dreadful and great darkness fell upon him. Then the LORD said to Abram, 'Know for certain that your offspring will be sojourners in a land that is not theirs and will be servants there, and they will be afflicted for four hundred years. But I will bring judgment on the nation that they serve, and afterward they shall come out with great possessions.'"* (Gen. 15:12–14)

---

[42] Umberto Cassuto. "A Commentary on the Book of Genesis, Part Two, From Noah to Abraham" Translated by Israel Abrahams (Jerusalem: Magnes Press 1964) 354

[43] By passing through the pieces HaShem takes sole responsibility for fulfilling the terms of the covenant. The custom was for both parties to pass through the pieces, thus binding themselves by imprecation to maintain covenant fidelity. See, Jer. 34:18,19.

The descendants Abraham longed for would eventually inherit the land HaShem promised Abraham, but in HaShem's plan they would first be required to endure 400 years of servitude.[44] Their servitude would be recompensed. HaShem would judge the nation that enslaved them (Egypt), and bring them out of slavery with great possessions.

This promise is repeated to Moses at his encounter with HaShem at the burning bush. Not only does HaShem promise to deliver His people, but the wages withheld from Israel for 400 years of servitude would be paid to them in full (Exod. 3:21). Indeed, according to the promise first made to Abraham in Genesis 15, and later repeated to Moses at the burning bush, when Israel left the land they left with great wealth:

> *"The people of Israel had also done as Moses told them, for they had asked the Egyptians for silver and gold jewelry and for clothing. And the LORD had given the people favor in the sight of the Egyptians, so that they let them have what they asked. Thus they plundered the Egyptians."*
> (Exod. 12:35–36)

These two examples in the Torah of Israel obtaining wealth, contrast against one another. One could reckon Israel's plundering of the Egyptians as recompense, an act in keeping with divine justice. The Egyptians not only pay the

---

[44] The delay of 430 years was required in order to satisfy the necessary conditions to bring judgment on the inhabitants of Canaan. "And they shall come back here in the fourth generation, for the iniquity of the Amorites is not yet complete." (Gen. 15:16)

consequences for Pharaoh's disobedience to release Israel from slavery but also pay Israel the wages that had been owed them for 400 years of servitude. But Abraham can make no such claim. Despite his deceitfulness, on two occasions two Gentile kings bless him.

Abraham's reception of wealth gives added meaning to Paul's comment in Romans 4:4,[45] "Now to the one who works, his wages are not counted as a gift but as his due" (Rom. 4:4). Perhaps Israel's wages received by the Egyptians could be understood as their due, but Abraham's wealth at the hand of Pharaoh and Abimelech was the gracious gift of HaShem, and not even a reward for faithfulness. Abraham received the blessing despite his lack of faith in HaShem's promise.

What connects these contrasting events together is the wealth of the nations distributed to Israel to fulfill HaShem's purposes. This is just the beginning of a pattern that extends throughout the Hebrew Scriptures. My friend and mentor, Eitan Shishkoff wrote an excellent book that delves into this topic.[46] I would recommend Eitan's book to you, in my opinion, it is in some ways a companion volume to this book, as it also deals with the relationship between Jews and Gentiles for the fulfillment of God's purposes, though from a slightly different perspective.

Among his many valuable insights, Eitan goes into detail about how the dynamic of Gentile giving to Israel is patterned throughout the Hebrew Scriptures. He cites the example of

---

[45] To be clear, Romans 4:4 is about receiving justification by faith not by works.
[46] Eitan Shishkoff. "What About Us?" (Bedford, TX: Burkhart Books, 2013)

Hiram contributing the building materials for Solomon's temple as an example of Jew and Gentile cooperation to fulfill the purposes of God.[47] The same pattern is repeated with Cyrus bankrolling Zerubbabel to return to Jerusalem and re-build the temple and Artaxerxes bankrolling Nehemiah to restore Jerusalem's walls.[48]

Isaiah prophesies that this same pattern of Gentile wealth bestowed upon Israel will accompany Israel's restoration:

> *Then you shall see and be radiant; your heart shall thrill and exult, because the abundance of the sea shall be turned to you, the wealth of the nations shall come to you. A multitude of camels shall cover you, the young camels of Midian and Ephah; all those from Sheba shall come. ... For the coastlands shall hope for me, the ships of Tarshish first, to bring your children from afar, their silver and gold with them, for the name of the LORD your God, and for the Holy One of Israel, because he has made you beautiful. Foreigners shall build up your walls, and their kings shall minister to you...Your gates shall be open continually; day and night they shall not be shut, that people may bring to you the wealth of the nations, with their kings led in procession.* (Isa. 60:5–11)

This beautiful imagery depicts Israel returning from exile, accompanied by the abundance of the seas, gold and silver, precious spices, flocks and building materials — the wealth of

---

[47] Ibid. 18
[48] Ibid. 21-23

the nations bestowed on Israel for her physical restoration. The plundering of the Egyptians and the outlay of material support from Gentile rulers for Jerusalem and the Temple is a foreshadowing of extravagant wealth from the nations bestowed upon Israel on her return from exile.

The pattern of Gentile wealth being distributed to Israel continues in the Apostolic Writings. Following Peter's breakthrough witness to Cornelius the Gentile, and the subsequent Jerusalem church's breakthrough revelation that *"to the Gentiles also God has granted repentance that leads to life"* (Acts 11:18); we see a shift in how the Gospel expands into the world.[49] Whereas previously, Jewish evangelists in the diaspora proclaimed the Gospel *"to no one except Jews"* (Acts 11:19), following these events in Antioch, some Jewish evangelists begin proclaiming the Gospel among the Gentiles (Acts 11:20).

The fruit of this evangelism was *"a great number [of Gentiles] who believed turned to the Lord"* (Acts 11:21). Though Antioch had Jewish members of the congregation, this was the first church with a predominantly Gentile constituency. Our discussion of Acts 15 (chapter one) showed that the church in Antioch looked to Jerusalem for spiritual authority. Indeed, when the Elders in Jerusalem got news of this new work in Antioch they sent Barnabas to disciple them (Acts 11:22). Later, prophets came down from Jerusalem to encourage the Antioch believers.[50]

---

[49] See Chapter One, "Paul's Revelation of the Gospel" for a more in depth look at Peter, Cornelius and the impact of their encounter.

[50] Acts 11:26 states that the still pagan Antioch society at large was the first group in the empire to designate these Gentile believers as Christians.

Agabus was one such prophet. He enters the story again in Acts 21, warning Paul that danger awaited him in Jerusalem (Acts 21:10,11). In chapter 11, he accurately predicts that a famine would soon blight the whole Roman world (Acts 11:28). The response of these first Gentile believers in Antioch is curious. We have Joseph's story as a precedent. Joseph received the revelation that Pharaoh's unusual dream about blighted cattle and wheat is confirmation that a seven year famine will descend upon Egypt. Filled with wisdom, Joseph advises Pharaoh to gather the country's resources so as to ride out the famine years that are coming.

Agabus warns the church in Antioch that this famine will cover the whole Roman world. That is, Antioch itself is headed for a famine. The wise response would be for the Antioch church to follow Joseph's counsel and gather their resources to ride out the famine coming their way. They do gather their resources but then they put an unlikely twist on their preparations:

"And one of them named Agabus stood up and foretold by the Spirit that there would be a great famine over all the world (this took place in the days of Claudius). So the disciples determined, every one according to his ability, to send relief to the brothers living in Judea. And they did so, sending it to the elders by the hand of Barnabas and Saul." (Acts 11:28–30)

This church of Gentiles, learning the ways of the Lord from Jewish leaders Barnabas and Saul, gathered their resources. But, instead of holding on to them to hedge against the famine, they determine to send these resources to the Jewish church in Judea. Agabus did not say there was going to be a famine in Judea only. He said the whole Roman world — which included Antioch. Why did this first Gentile congregation single out the believers in Judea as recipients of famine relief? Surely this was not just a practical decision. Something besides humanitarian concern was at work here. Otherwise Judea would not have been singled out as the object of their beneficence.

The church in Antioch's response to the famine follows the pattern of Gentile material support for Israel, a pattern beginning with Abraham and following throughout Israel's history. Later, Paul explains to the church in Rome that this is an obligation of the Gentile church:

> *"But now I am going to Jerusalem to minister to the saints. For it pleased those from Macedonia and Achaia to make a certain contribution for the poor among the saints who are in Jerusalem. It pleased them indeed, and they are their debtors. For if the Gentiles have been partakers of their spiritual things, their duty is also to minister to them in material things."* (Rom. 15:25–27 NKJV)

Perhaps Paul taught this principle to the church in Antioch before he wrote it to the Romans. This is quite possible, as Paul had been teaching in Antioch for at least a year (Acts 11:26). We cannot make this claim with certainty, but the Antioch believers explicitly follow this teaching. In Romans 15, Paul develops a teaching on Gentile giving towards Israel that has the foundation of scriptural precedent from the Hebrew Scriptures and at least the historical example of the first Gentile congregation in Antioch.

In Romans 15, Paul refers to churches in Macedonia and Achaia. Macedonia and Achaia are Roman provinces. Philippi was the chief city in Macedonia and Corinth the chief city in Achaia.[51] Paul informed the Romans that he was on his way to Jerusalem with an offering for the church in Jerusalem. No famine was in view here but the church in Philippi and Corinth were following the precedent established by Antioch. Paul wants the Roman church to know that this offering is not just an example of goodwill and generosity, nor even a kind gesture that follows the Antioch example. These churches are obeying a spiritual principle.

Israel, the covenant people of God have shared their spiritual riches with the Gentiles. Through the Messiah of Israel the family has expanded to include the nations. Earlier Paul explained to the Romans that this inclusion into God's family was "riches" for the world and the nations (Rom. 11:12). Now, the recipients of these spiritual riches were to share their material wealth as a reciprocal blessing.

I think it is important that this precedent did not start with Antioch but carries through the whole witness of scripture. However, Paul is the first scripture author to provide an explanation of the principle previously only expressed by example.[52]

---

[51] See Acts 16:12 and Acts 18:1,12

[52] In addition, Isaiah 60:5 predicts that the nations will bestow their wealth to Israel.

Paul uses the words "debtor and owe"[53] words that don't fit well with Paul's other teachings on giving. II Corinthians 8,9 provide the back-story for Paul's teaching on giving in Romans 15. Paul is on his way to Corinth. He informs the Corinthians that he has already received a generous offering from the Philippians for the church in Jerusalem.[54] Having received a promise a year earlier from the Corinthians (2 Cor. 8:10), that they were eager to contribute to this benevolence, Paul sends Titus and a companion ahead of him to Corinth to prepare the church to participate in this giving (2 Cor. 8:23,24).

Paul is not above reminding the Corinthians that they had already promised to give and that he had relayed their intentions to the believers in Philippi. He wants to make sure they are ready when he arrives. He provokes them to fulfill what they had promised by appealing to their conscience. How embarrassed both Paul and the Corinthians would be if a member of the church in Philippi accompanied him to Corinth and discovered they had not fulfilled their pledge.[55] Though not saying it directly, Paul is communicating that the Corinthians are in fact obligated to follow through with a generous financial gift for the church in Jerusalem.

But this language of obligation is secondary to the central message. Prior to chapter 15, Romans spells out how God has bestowed lavish generosity to the Gentiles. They have become children of Abraham by exercising the faith of Abraham.

---

[53] ὀφειλέτης *ofeiletace* literally a debtor and ὀφείλω *ofeielo literally to owe*
[54] In 2 Corinthians Paul uses the term "saints" (8:4). However, it is clear the church in Jerusalem is in view (Rom. 15:26).
[55] 2 Cor. 9:1-4

Through Yeshua's death and resurrection all of us in Mes[s] have died to sin and been raised to newness of life. God placed His Holy Spirit in us, bearing witness to our spirits that we are children of God. Most of us who have any familiarity with Paul's letter to the Romans are familiar with these wonderful promises of eternal life and God's boundless love.

In chapter five we covered in great detail that this lavish grace was at the expense of the Jewish people. It is through Israel's trespass that salvation came to the Gentiles (Rom. 11:11). Israel's rejection meant reconciliation for the world (Rom. 11:15), Jewish branches were broken off to make room for Gentile branches to be grafted in (Rom. 11:17). There is no doubt that the Gentiles have received spiritual blessings from Israel.

More than this, it is Yeshua's generosity that compels us to give Him our all, including our finances. Messiah Yeshua, though God's appointed ruler for the world and the eternal Son of God dwelling in heavenly glory, left his majestic estate and humbled himself to become a man and suffer death on a Roman cross. As Paul reminds the Corinthians, *"For you know the grace of our Lord Jesus Christ, that though he was rich, yet for your sake he became poor, so that you by his poverty might become rich"* (2 Cor. 8:9). God's generosity in Messiah is so vast that any giving on our part can only be meager in comparison.

God loves a cheerful giver because a cheerful giver happily accepts the obligation to give in response to God's tremendous generosity. The church in Antioch gladly accepted this obligation, as did the church in Philippi and, perhaps because of a little prodding, so did the church in Corinth. God expects generous sowing because He has already sown the most generous seed possible, the life of His son.[56]

This general rule of giving from the Gentile churches to the believers in Israel is further borne out by Paul's original instructions to the Corinthians. In 1 Corinthians 16, Paul addresses the Corinthians' concern about the correct protocol for taking up offerings in the church.[57] Paul explains that the instructions he is about to impart he has already explained to the churches in Galatia. On the *"first day of every week"* (1 Cor. 16:2), according to his or her ability, each member of the church is to put some money aside in anticipation of Paul's arrival. After Paul arrives he will either send a Corinthian delegation ahead of him, or he will accompany them on their journey to Jerusalem to distribute their collection for the church there.

This was a standard practice Paul had already established for the churches in Galatia. The Corinthians were concerned enough about doing this correctly that they asked Paul for instructions. The gist of Paul's instructions was this: All the Corinthian believers were to participate and the recipients of this collection were the Jewish believers in Jerusalem.

Giving is a sensitive topic. There is always the potential for greed and manipulation to mar what is a very tangible expression of faith. Paul's writings on the subject emphasize

---

[56] John 12:24

[57] 1 Corinthians 16:1 begins with the phrase "Now concerning" [Gk. *peri de*]. This is the fifth of six sections of the letter (7:1, 25; 8:1; 12:1; 16:1, 12) that use this phrase to begin Paul's explanation of the given topic. Most commentators agree that these refer to matters that the Corinthians had previously written about to Paul. See, Gordon D. Fee. "The First Epistle To The Corinthians," The New International Commentary On The New Testament (Grand Rapids, MI: Eerdmans, 1987), 266,267

that giving should never be associated with coercion or enriching some at the expense of others. Rather, giving is to be what in its pure sense it has always been, a tangible expression of worship motivated by gratitude and accompanied by faith.

The exchange between spiritual and material blessing is a practical expression of mutual blessing. In chapter two I reviewed how mutual blessing is the intended relational dynamic between Israel and the nations. The blessings bestowed on Israel are always with the nations in view. As the nations are blessed the blessings flow back to Israel. As these blessings continue the cycle ramps up in a beautiful expanding spiral of blessing.

The call to the Gentiles to bestow material blessing to Israel is not a plundering of the one for the benefit of the other. It is the reciprocal response for blessings already received. In a sense, it is the necessary response to balance out the equation of reciprocity but it does not end there. The blessings flow back and forth in mutuality. As the church in the nations takes up this call to contribute financial blessing to Israel, the blessings flow back to the church in the nations, not only spiritual blessings received from the Jewish people but also, in an abounding grace that equips the church in the nations with sufficient provision for every good work. Usually when God's people are encouraged to give, two well known Pauline passages are employed:

> *"And God is able to make all grace abound to you, so that having all sufficiency in all things at all times, you may abound in every good work."* (2 Cor. 9:8)

"And my God will supply every need of yours according to his riches in glory in Christ Jesus." (Phil. 4:19)

There is no coincidence that these words of encouragement of God's faithfulness to meet our material and financial needs are addressed to the two churches who generously gave of their material goods to bless the Jewish household of faith. In light of all God has done for all of us, both Jew and Gentile, the truth of obligation is transformed into loving gratitude. May we hear the Holy Spirit speaking through Paul's words for the church in the nations to once again *"excel in this act of grace also."*

Gentile material wealth is in keeping with the prophetic mandate of Isaiah 60, the precedent set by example through the Exodus, the building of both temples, and the Apostolic foundation laid by Paul and embraced by the Gentile churches under his Apostolic care and authority.

Regrettably, this foundation did not continue to grow with the expansion of the church in the nations. To the contrary, though Paul was eager for the Corinthians, so enriched by the grace of God to add this grace also, the church in the nations failed to recognize this calling, and even as Paul explained, this obligation to sow materially into the household of faith in Israel. Unlike previous generations, we now, like those first Gentile churches have the opportunity to materially bless the Jewish church in Israel. Messianic faith has been revived in Jerusalem and throughout Israel.

Often, we long to recover the purity, vitality and faith of the early church. We look to the example set in the Book of

Acts as the model for what the believing community is to look like and how we are to function. Usually we emphasize the wonderful miracles and evangelistic revivals described in Acts. We have a sense that as it was in the beginning so it will be in the end, but on an even greater scale.

I too, long for an increase in a miraculous demonstration of God's love and power, and to see the church expand throughout the nations. Our opportunity to engage in the material giving set out by Paul in Romans 15:25-27 is a practical opportunity for present day believers in the nations to enter into a grace afforded those first Gentile believers. Does your heart burn to see the revivals of the Book of Acts repeated in our day? Will you enter into this grace of sowing finances into the Messianic community of Israel, as exemplified by the Gentile churches recorded in the Book of Acts?

Response: Our Abundant Wealth

Peg Byars, Communications Director, Return Ministries.

I first met Peg in 2001 when she served as the administrator organizing a large delegation of Canadian Christians to Israel. Peg is a woman of passion, energy and integrity. She came to the Lord later in life but has used the most of every opportunity given her. She serves as the Communications Director for Return Ministries, a Canadian based Christian Zionist ministry. (MS)

My name is Peg Byars and I am 78 years young. I came to faith in 1984 at the age of 45. At that time I was an executive at one of Canada's large banks. Ten years later I retired from the banking world and began a new adventure as an intercessory prayer leader. My focus began with my own city but quickly, stirred by a passion to obey Yeshua's command to be His witness, expanded out to the nations of the world. I led several teams of intercessors on international assignments. As the Lord has continued to lead me on my journey, my prayer burden for the world has led me to narrow my focus once again onto a singular burden for the "Apple of God's eye," the Jewish people. Now, as a director with Return Ministries, and having journeyed to Israel over 20 times, sowing into projects that are bringing about the restoration of Israel, I am committed with everything that is in me to be a contributing part of the "wealth of the Gentiles" towards Israel's restoration.

Marty began his chapter by quoting from Isaiah 60 about the wealth of the Gentiles being gathered to Israel. The Hebrew word translated In Isaiah 60:5 as wealth is *hayil.* This is the same word that is often translated in the Hebrew Scriptures as army. According to the Brown Driver Briggs Hebrew/English Lexicon[58] this word can also be translated as strength, ability, worth, valour, and efficiency. Wealth is so much more in Hebrew thought than I first imagined. Therefore, we in the nations have a multitude of opportunities to fulfill our role to give of our wealth. Listen to God's call to us:

And they shall rebuild the old ruins,
They shall raise up the former desolations,
And they shall repair the ruined cities,
The desolations of many generations.
Strangers shall stand and feed your flocks,
And the sons of the foreigner shall be your plowmen
and your vinedressers.
But you shall be named the priests of the LORD,
They shall call you the servants of our God.
You shall eat the riches (wealth) of the Gentiles,

---

[58]A Hebrew and English Lexicon of the Old Testament (BDB complete) by Francis Brown, S.R. Driver, and Charles A. Briggs
Original electronic text copyright © Scribe, Inc., Dania Beach, Florida USA Used by permission.
Electronic text corrected, hypertexted, and prepared by OakTree Software, Inc. Version 4.3

And in their glory you shall boast.
Instead of your shame you shall have double honor,
And instead of confusion they shall rejoice in their
portion. Therefore in their land they shall possess
double; Everlasting joy shall be theirs. (Isa. 61:4-7)

We are seeing a direct fulfillment of these words in our day. Every year hundreds of Gentile volunteers come to the vineyards and orchards of Judea and Samaria - to plant, prune and reap the ever-increasing harvests of grapes, olives and pomegranates in the heartland of Israel. Their volunteer contributions are bringing in millions of shekels in revenue for the welfare of these hard working Israeli farmers.

In the process of assisting the vineyard owners to accomplish their overwhelming tasks, the wealth of these Gentiles is contributing to the fulfillment of Amos 9:13-15:

"Behold, the days are coming," declares the LORD, "when
the plowman will overtake the reaper and the treader of
grapes him who sows seed; when the mountains will drip
with sweet wine and all the hills will be dissolved. Also I
will restore the captivity of My people Israel, and they
will rebuild the ruined cities and live in them; they will
also plant vineyards and drink their wine, and make
gardens and eat their fruit. I will also plant them on
their land, and they will not again be rooted out of their
land which I have given them," says the LORD your God.

So what is the blessing for the Gentile in all this? When Jew and Gentile work together to fulfill God's covenant promises, His holy name is sanctified. And when His name is once more hallowed in Israel by the Jews returning from the nations, His blessings begin to pour out - not just on Israel, but the whole world. The Father has been so patient for us to step fully into our role so He can unfold His sovereign plan.

There are specific instructions in the Scriptures regarding our role as Gentiles towards the Jewish people. We are to comfort and speak kindly to them (Isa. 40:1-2); carry them home (Isa. 49:22); and serve them (Isa. 14:1-2). And as we do obey these instructions another layer of God's promises is activated:

1) All nations will know He is the LORD (Ezek. 36:23).
2) Aliyah, reconciliation and redemption of the Jewish people takes place (Ezek. 36:24-28).
3) Resurrection power is released upon the whole world! (Rom. 11:15).

Surely the prospect of any one of these promises coming to pass should thrill our hearts and activate our actions, but the culmination is even greater – the coming of Messiah, Yeshua, our King. He is the restorer of all things as the Apostle Peter's second sermon declares:

But those things which God foretold by the mouth of all His prophets, that the Christ would suffer, He has thus fulfilled. Repent therefore and be converted, that your sins may be blotted out, so that times of refreshing may come from the presence of the Lord, and that He may send Jesus Christ, who was preached to you before, whom heaven must receive until the times of restoration of all things, which God has spoken by the mouth of all His holy prophets since the world began. (Acts 3:18-21)

In the closing words of chapter 6, Marty has set before us a challenge and a charge:

"Our opportunity to engage in the material giving set out by Paul in Romans 15:25-27 is a practical opportunity for present day believers in the nations to enter into a grace afforded those first Gentile believers. Does your heart burn to see the revivals of the Book of Acts repeated in our day? Will you enter into this grace of sowing finances into the Messianic community of Israel as exemplified by the Gentile churches recorded in the Book of Acts?"

I believe God is awaking the remnant in the body of Christ in the western world to participate in this challenge. Here is another example of some of the amazing initiatives going on in our world to bless Israel.

When a man in the New Brunswick, Canada heard God say, "I want you to give ten white trucks to Israel" he responded, "Yes, Lord." But the Father then laid down a weighty condition; that he use this act of generosity to challenge Canadians all across the country to love God and bless Israel with extravagant generosity.

What followed was a journey of God's grace. In the summer of 2015, 35 hardy souls travelled for 60 days in 10 white trucks, from Victoria, British Columbia to St. John's, Newfoundland conducting around 100 meetings through 10 provinces of Canada.

The Lord stirred the hearts of Canadians to give extravagantly, well beyond what the organizers had anticipated. People gave of their gold and silver, their personal heirlooms, even like Barnabas of old, selling property and donating the purchase price of the land. This was the answer to the Father's challenge to His condition – extravagant generosity - the ten white trucks became the largest offering baskets in history!

And what did Canadians receive? A greater understanding of God's covenant promises and His commitment to keep covenant with all that He promised to the Patriarchs. We have received tremendous testimonies of marriages strengthened, broken relationships restored, and parents and children being re-united. And the greatest blessing? God's name was hallowed in the midst of these faithful Canadian believers.

Some of the gold and silver has been melted down and made into Restoration Rings. These rings, inscribed in Hebrew with the words from Jeremiah 30:3, *"I will restore the fortunes of my people,"* have been given to Israelis who have given their lives to build the nation of Israel: Holocaust survivors, pioneers, soldiers and leaders from many backgrounds.

Compassion ministries in Israel are now driving vehicles that this humble New Brunswick car dealer has given in Yeshua's name. And back at home in New Brunswick, God is blessing him with the promise that revival is coming to the land. In the summer of 2016 he held 120 days of tent meetings on his property, exalting the name of our God and furthering the Kingdom. The Lord poured out His Spirit with signs and wonders, healings and lives redeemed.

Oh dear brothers and sisters in the Gentile body, it is time to get on God's calendar and His timetable. I believe we are entering the most crucial season in God's timetable since the death, resurrection and ascension of Yeshua the Messiah. He has ordained that Jew and Gentile are to work together. Put one hand in Ezekiel 36 and the other in Romans 11 and let's walk hand in hand into the times of refreshment and restoration so that the One New Man will come forth to welcome the coming of our Messiah to God's holy hill in Jerusalem.

We have the means to partner with the Father in the glorious preparation needed to welcome the King of kings and the Lord of lords. I call us to be the people of *hayil*: **strength, ability, worth, valour, efficiency, and wealth!** Rise up and take Marty's challenge. Find a way to express your love of God by blessing Israel. And *"Pray for the peace of Jerusalem; may they prosper who love you"* (Ps. 122:6).

The Conclusion of the Matter

Yeshua, One New Man

The ultimate purpose set forth in Messiah is that all things both in heaven and earth will be gathered together in him (Eph. 1:9,10). Everything begins and ends with Messiah:

> *"He is the image of the invisible God, the firstborn of all creation. For by him all things were created, in heaven and on earth, visible and invisible, whether thrones or dominions or rulers or authorities—all things were created through him and for him. And he is before all things, and in him all things hold together. And he is the head of the body, the church. He is the beginning, the firstborn from the dead, that in everything he might be preeminent. For in him all the fullness of God was pleased to dwell, and through him to reconcile to himself all things, whether on earth or in heaven, making peace by the blood of his cross."* (Col. 1:15–20)

He is preeminent in every way. It is through Messiah Yeshua that the world was made and it is through Messiah Yeshua that the word is redeemed. All things are gathered together in him (Eph. 1:10), and all things are reconciled together in him (Col. 1:20). When we speak of One New Man as a paradigm for the body of Messiah, ultimately, we are talking about the person of Messiah himself. He is *the head of the body* (Col. 1:18). Together as Jew and Gentile, we are being made as One New Man in Messiah because Messiah Himself is One New Man.

In chapter 2, I discussed Yeshua's mandate with respect to both Israel and the Gentiles. Isaiah 49 sets out that the Messiah was born as HaShem's servant to restore the tribes of Israel and to be a light to the Gentiles (Isa. 49:5,6). However, Yeshua is more than just the servant tasked with fulfilling the Father's will for Jew and Gentile. He is the identification of both Jew and Gentile. He is the representative head of Israel and the representative head of humanity, and by extension therefore, of all the nations.

Yeshua is King of the Jews. He is the head of the Israel as the promised son of David whose rule would extend forever:

"When your days are fulfilled to walk with your fathers, I will raise up your offspring after you, one of your own sons, and I will establish his kingdom. He shall build a house for me, and I will establish his throne forever. I will be to him a father, and he shall be to me a son. I will not take my steadfast love from him, as I took it from him who was before you, but I will confirm him in my house and in my kingdom forever, and his throne shall be established forever."' (1 Chron. 17:11–14)

According to the covenant HaShem made with David, David's line would continue into perpetuity (2 Sam. 7:16).

The corresponding 1 Chronicles passage (1 Chron. 17), emphasizes that this eternal rule would be through one particular descendant. The angel Gabriel's announcement to Miriam echoes this same promise:

> *"He will be great, and will be called the Son of the Highest; and the Lord God will give Him the throne of His father David. And He will reign over the house of Jacob forever, and of His kingdom there will be no end."* (Luke 1:32,33)

Yeshua is the promised descendant of David who will rule over *"the House of Jacob forever"* (Luke 1:33). Of all the wonderful attributes and qualities of Yeshua we sometimes overlook His most obvious feature. Yeshua is a King. The word "Messiah" or Christ is not Yeshua's last name, but the fitting epithet to His core characteristic. Yeshua is the anointed one, anointed to be King. Gabriel's announcement declares, *"He will be called the Son of the Highest"* (Luke 1:32). This pronouncement's most immediate meaning is not a Trinitarian formulation but a hearkening back to God's promise to David regarding his heir, *"I will be His Father, and He shall be my Son"* (1Chron. 17:13).

Psalm two reiterates this same promise; *"'I have set My king on My holy hill of Zion'. I will declare the decree: The LORD said to me, 'You are My Son, today I have begotten you'"* (Ps. 2:6,7). The "decree" referenced here is the word spoken to David of the heir who would come from his line whose *"throne will be established forever"* (I Chron.17:14). This is the same promise Gabriel makes to Miriam - Yeshua is the long awaited king who will sit on David's throne forever. As King, Yeshua not only rules over Israel, he is the representative head of the nation.

Israel is God's son (Exod. 4:22,23), as representative head of the nation, the king of Israel becomes God's son. The King represents the nation before HaShem. When Israel's king did right, the nation was blessed. Likewise, when the king did evil, the nation was judged. There were some kings who did right (most did evil), but even Israel's, and later, Judah's best kings fell short. None of them, not David, not Solomon, not Hezekiah nor Josiah fulfilled the mandate as Israel's king so as to rule over the nation forever. Only Yeshua, Israel's king, who absolutely obeyed Israel's God, fulfilled the expectations set out in HaShem's promise to David. Therefore, Yeshua's mandate is to restore the tribes of Israel is not just a mandated task; he restores Israel because he is, in a sense the embodiment of Israel, the promised offspring of David who rules over Jacob forever.

Yeshua is also the heir to another king. Adam was given the mandate to rule (Gen.1:26). Adam is never addressed as king but he fits the definition. A king rules over a realm. In Adam's case, the realm he was given authority to rule over was the entire planet. And just as Yeshua is the embodiment of Israel, so Adam is the embodiment of the human race. That is why Paul explains that on account of Adam's sin, sin and death *spread to all men because all sinned*" (Rom. 5:12). Because Adam is the embodiment of the human race, we are all in Adam and therefore Adam's sin, and the consequences thereof pass on to all of us.

The issue for all of Israel's (and later Judah's) kings was the same as it was for king Adam. The one to whom HaShem gives authority to rule is required to obey HaShem completely. As the new representative head of the human race, the last Adam (1 Cor. 15:45), Yeshua, succeeded where the first Adam failed. Whereas the first Adam was disobedient and therefore brought sin and death upon all, Yeshua, the last Adam was obedient to the point of death and brought the prospect of salvation to all (Rom. 5:18).

Likewise, as the Son of David, Yeshua succeeds where Solomon and all who came after did not. All who came before Yeshua, because of their sin, were not worthy to rule over the house of Jacob forever. Yeshua, the son of God obeyed his Heavenly Father in all things - even to the point of death, was crucified as *"King of the Jews."* Within this one appointed ruler is the embodiment of Israel, because he is Israel's eternal king and also the embodiment of all the nations, because he is the last Adam. We are in the process of being formed as One New Man because Yeshua himself is One New Man.

The magnitude of our identification in the King of Israel/Last Adam is that Yeshua, the perfectly obedient man is at the same time, the Lord from heaven, the image of the invisible God, who made all things, who is before all things, who holds together all things, *"all things were created through him and for him"* (Col. 1:16). All who are in Yeshua, whether Jew or Gentle, receive their identification in him as the representative head of both Israel and the nations. He is the perfect man who obeyed HaShem where others tasked with the same (Adam, and later Israel's kings) all failed. Yet, this perfect man who represents us all, and with us all shares his

181

inheritance (Rom. 8:17); indeed, Yeshua, who has made the Gentiles fellow heirs with Israel (Eph. 3:6), is God Himself. This is the greatest mystery of all. In Yeshua, both Jew and Gentile are made heirs together with Messiah (Rom. 8:17), who as the divine Son is the heir of all things.

Yeshua, on the eve of his death, that final act of obedience that demonstrated his conferred authority as HaShem's ruler (Phil. 2:8-11), devoted his longest recorded prayer - not for himself but for his followers. Yeshua's passion for His disciples is that they would be one even as He and the Father are one. The magnitude of Yeshua's request is unparalleled by any other prayer. The Father and Son enjoy perfect oneness. There is no strife between them, no misunderstanding, and no insecurity. The Father loves the Son with absolute love and the Son obeys the Father with absolute obedience. This divine oneness is so far above and beyond my own comprehension. How can I, or any human being truly describe the oneness between the Father and Son?

But the Son knew of what He was asking. He was the only human being who could truly comprehend the portent of His words. His hour had come. He was soon to lay down His life as the Lamb of God who takes away the sin of the world. The Son who always obeys the father knew *"It was the will of the LORD to crush him"* (Isaiah 53:10a). The Son's answer to this daunting reality was *"Nevertheless, not my will but your will be done."* Isaiah's prophetic response to the servant Messiah being crushed according to HaShem's will concludes, *"When his soul makes an offering for guilt, he shall see his offspring; he shall prolong his days; the will of the LORD shall prosper in his hand. Out of the anguish of his soul he shall see and be satisfied"* (Isa. 53:10–11).

Yeshua knew that despite the price He would pay, in the end he would see the anguish, or the travail of his soul and be satisfied. All that the Son has desired the Father will fulfill. We who so easily divide into factions will be one, even as Yeshua is one with the Father.

A great repair is required in order for this to happen. The Body of Messiah has yet to attain anything like the unity between Father and Son. But in the beginning we did have a unity that has not been rivalled by any generation since. A unity has been fractured. The initial breach was not between Catholic and Protestant, not between Evangelical and Charismatic not even between The Eastern and Western Orthodoxies. The original schism was between the church of the circumcision and the church of the uncircumcision, in modern parlance, between Messianic Jews and Gentile Christians.

This book has not delved into church history and all the ways the church over the centuries distanced itself from its connection to Israel and the Jewish people. The church adopted the view that it was the new Israel and therefore saw no interest in maintaining a connection to those whom they understood to be under a curse and soon to cease from history. As we have discussed this is not consistent with the testimony of scripture.

I once shared a platform with a wonderful Nigerian preacher. Using Yeshua's words to the Ephesian church in Revelation chapter 2, he explained that one could define repentance as going back to where you started. The Ephesians had lost their first love. Yeshua's command to them was, *"Remember therefore from where you have fallen; repent, and do the works you did at first"* (Rev. 2:5). In order for the Ephesians to repent they had to go back to the place from where they first fell. They had to address that first transgression that set them off course.

Today, we have the same task. We cannot begin to address the matter of disunity plaguing the church without going back to the place from where we have fallen. All the good intentions, public displays of unity and ecumenical efforts will not achieve the goal without addressing that first schism that set the course of disunity we have tracked on ever since.

According to Isaiah 53, Yeshua offered Himself as the sacrifice for sin to justify many. According to Ephesians 2&3, He did so to make One New Man composed of Jew and Gentile, now joint heirs together in Messiah. This is the desire of His soul — to see us become one. Because the Son has obeyed the Father, no matter how gargantuan the task may seem to us, the Father will grant the Son the desire of His heart. He will see the labor of His soul and be satisfied.

But, because we are joint heirs, Yeshua's reward for His obedience is also our reward. Not only so, He is our Lord, the head of the Body, the master we all love and obey. We have a vested interest in seeing our Lord's request fulfilled. Ultimately, the Father grants the Son's request but not with the joint heirs watching passively from the sidelines. Our part is to remember from where we have fallen and do the works we did at first.

In the beginning, the Body of Messiah in the nations honoured and cherished the church in Judea. They looked to those Jewish leaders as the chief delegated authority of the Messiah. When they had a dispute they could not resolve, they went to Jerusalem to receive an answer. When they had prophetic warning of a worldwide famine to come, they first ensured the church in Judea would be looked after. The chief apostle among the church in the nations gathered resources from those churches to bring back to Jerusalem, not in order that Jewish believers could be enriched at the expense of Gentile believers, but to ensure mutual blessing according to the pattern Messiah had determined.

Today, for the first time in over 1,800 years the Body of Messiah has the opportunity to return from whence we have fallen. In just the last 50 or so years the church of the circumcision has risen again from the ashes of history. Israel is back in the land promised to them by covenant and Messianic faith has been renewed in the land of Israel. Unlike previous generations, we are no longer hampered by circumstances. It is Messiah who creates One New Man but we are the generation that can avail ourselves of this opportunity. May the Father, who will fulfill the desires of the Son, grant us the grace, wisdom, power and humility to return from whence we have fallen, to restore the breach that shattered the relationship between Jew and Gentile in Messiah, and make us truly One New Man. This is our Lord's great request, may it move us with all our heart soul and strength.

CONTRIBUTORS

Rick Barker is lead pastor at Cariboo Christian Life Fellowship, 108 Mile Ranch, British Columbia, Canada. www.cclf.ca

Peg Byars is communications director for Return Ministries, Bright, Ontario, Canada. www.return.co.il

Dean Bye is executive director of Return Ministries, Bright, Ontario, Canada.

Joe Campbell is a minister at large, London Ontario. Joe serves as a pastor to the Return Ministries base staff.

Ernie Culley is the pastor of Ahava Life Center, Vancouver, British Columbia, Canada. www.lifecenter.ca

Sharon Hayton is the executive director of CMJ Canada, Victoria, British Columba, Canada. www.cmjcanada.ca

Eitan Shishkoff is the executive director of Tents of Mercy, a network of messianic ministries in Galilee, Israel. www.tentsofmercy.org

About the Author

Marty Shoub is an itinerant Bible teacher currently serving as an associate with Return Ministries and as the Canadian representative of Tikkun Ministries International. www.tikkunministries.org. Martin also serves as the co-pastor of Ahava Life Center, Vancouver, British Colombia, Canada.

Marty Shoub graduated with a BA honours in theology from Briercrest College in 1989 and a Masters of Jewish Studies from Messianic Jewish Theological Institute in 2015. Marty is a co-leader of the Loving God Blessing Israel initiative. www.lovinggodblessingisrael.com.

You can contact the author at:
MartyShoub@tikkuninternational.org